…jima Shinichi (ed.), *Masterpieces Selected from the Ukiyoye School, Volume V* (Tokyo: Shimbi Shoin, 1909)

Opposite middle. Fig. 6. A Japanese woman holding a white fan next to her face, unidentified photographer, before 1921, Yokohama *shashin* print

Opposite right. Fig. 7. *The Pink Kimono*, E. A. Hornel, *c.*1921–25, oil on canvas

Left. Fig. 8. Myanmar women in a market place, E. A. Hornel, *c.*1922–27, oil on canvas

sition of many of the Yokohama *shashin* prints that Hornel collected is mirrored in the composition of a number of his paintings.[5] He would paint full scenes and then crop them, as if taking a snapshot of the most visually appealing area. Against the frenzied, blurred backgrounds of his paintings, the faces and hands stand out, painted with almost photographic veracity.

The exploration of Hornel's photographic collection in *From Camera to Canvas* also reveals a more challenging hinterland to his paintings. While his hundreds of photographs of Scottish girls (brought to his studio by their mothers and chaperoned by his sister Elizabeth) are only discomfiting to a modern eye, many of those he took of girls and young women in Sri Lanka and Japan appear intimate or intrusive.

The exact status of the Japanese women he saw, and collected photographs of, seems to have mattered little to Hornel. While he

Above. Fig. 9. Two Kirkcudbright girls lying on the grass, with a third person reaching towards them, attributed to E. A. Hornel, between *c.*1890 and 1909, glass plate negative

Right. Fig. 10. A Kirkcudbright girl in a black dress facing away from the camera in front of a canvas, attributed to E. A. Hornel, *c.*1906–10, glass plate negative

Far right. Fig. 11. A Kirkcudbright girl in front of a rug in the studio at Broughton House, attributed to E. A. Hornel, *c.*1906–10, glass plate negative

certainly spent time with *geisha*[6] while in Japan, not all the women whose photos he collected (and subsequently used as direct models for his paintings) were *geisha*. However, the titles of his paintings frequently refer to Japanese women as '*geisha*' or '*geisha* girl'. While distinctions between *geisha*, *oiran* and other women wearing *kimono* were (and are) strictly delineated and vitally important in the real world, in his paintings these specific distinctions become blurred.[7]

Also problematic – although hardly atypical for the time – were his attitudes as a Westerner abroad experiencing 'the other', and his tendency to twist what he saw and the photographs he collected to fit his own romanticised ideas. The apparent authenticity of his Japanese scenes are in fact undercut by a plethora of inaccuracies, as Hornel relied on out-of-context photographs, ignored subtle nuances and modified poses and scenes to create more attractive (to Western eyes) compositions.[8] He packed his Japanese paintings with out-of-place symbols of Japan to enhance their commercial viability, and misunderstood or ignored Japanese etiquette.[9]

In Sri Lanka, his photographs ignore any nuance of identity among his subjects or, indeed, any sense of individual identity at all. His photographs of dancers in Myanmar later become conflated with

Below left. Fig. 12. A Japanese woman holding a fan towards the camera, unidentified photographer, probably 1893–94 or 1921, photographic print

Below middle. Fig. 13. A Japanese woman in a *kimono* holding a parasol and wearing *geta*, unidentified photographer, between c.1890 and 1921, Yokohama *shashin* print

Below right. Fig. 14. Two Japanese women from the back, showing off the patterns on their *kimono*, unidentified photographer, probably 1893–94 or 1921, photographic print

Above left. Fig. 15. A Myanmar woman holding a parasol, attributed to E. A. Hornel, 1920, glass plate negative

Above right. Fig. 16. A Sinhalese woman from the back holding a water pot, attributed to E. A. Hornel, 1907, glass plate negative (cracked)

Opposite left. Fig. 17. A Japanese woman holding a white fan below her chin, unidentified photographer, before 1921, Yokohama *shashin* print

Opposite right. Fig. 18. A Japanese woman in a *kimono*, E. A. Hornel, *c.*1921–25, oil on canvas

photos of Sri Lankan and Japanese women, to create paintings of 'Burmese' water carriers. Even the girls he photographed in Kirkcudbright were posed to fit an innocent, rural ideal rather than illustrate any individuality or contemporary reality.

Hornel's connection with Kirkcudbright was through his father, William L. Hornell (1822–1879).[10] Hornel himself was born in 1864 in the township of Bacchus Marsh, near Melbourne, Australia. His father and Yorkshire-born mother Ann (née Habbishaw, 1832–1906) had arrived in Australia in 1857 in search of a brighter future. The family lived in Australia for almost ten years, before returning to Kirkcudbright in 1866. Although Hornel travelled to Edinburgh and Antwerp to study art in the 1880s, he maintained his links with Kirkcudbright, eventually purchasing Broughton House there in 1900, where he lived until his death in 1933. He continued to travel extensively throughout his life to Myanmar, Sri Lanka, Japan, Canada, the USA and back to Australia.

Japan was to be particularly significant for Hornel. He visited twice, first for 13 months in 1893–94 with friend and fellow artist George Henry (1858–1943), and again in 1921 with his sister Elizabeth (1859–1950), affectionately known as Tizzy. It was his 1893–94 trip to Japan that turned his initial interest in photography into a fully fledged obsession. The visit, and the photographs he collected there, would completely change his way of seeing the world and his way of working. The chapters in this publication explore this transformation, but also set Hornel's painting process in a wider context.

While Hornel's family were travelling from Scotland to Australia and back again, painters in Europe such as Dante Gabriel Rossetti (1828–1882) were exploring the possibilities that the new medium of photography offered for their art. Alix Agret's chapter in this book introduces us to the artistic context – both European and specifically Scottish – that Hornel emerged from in the 1880s, before he first visited Japan. Agret also looks at attitudes to childhood and sensuality during this era, demonstrating how Hornel's photographs of Scottish girls fit into this context.

Jennifer Melville also contextualises Hornel's work by examining the influence that both the Scottish Colourists and the continental, Japan-inspired Post-Impressionists had on his work, before he first went to Japan. Melville demonstrates that as a result of living and studying in Antwerp from 1883 to 1885 – where he flourished after three disappointing years in Edinburgh[11] – Hornel's painting style began to change, becoming more expressive and colourful. It is possible that his experiences on the Continent (where painting and photography had long had a symbiotic relationship[12]), as well as his interactions with members of the 'Glasgow School' of artists and designers, also piqued his interest in photography. In retrospect, it is clear that the decade leading up to Hornel's first visit to Japan was instrumental in the paintings he produced upon his return from the country.

Hornel had an opportunity to engage directly with Japanese photography through the Photographic Society of Japan, whose members he helped to hang an exhibition of British photography shortly after his arrival in Japan. In his chapter, Luke Gartlan touches on the ongoing dialogue between Japanese and Western artists, which had been developing over the four decades before Hornel and Henry's visit. Gartlan also looks more closely at the importance of photography and painting networks, such as the Photographic Society of Japan, with regard to Hornel and Henry's engagement with the country, and their subsequent photographic collecting.

Opposite. Fig. 19. *Two Japanese Girls*, E. A. Hornel, *c.*1921–25, oil on canvas

Following on from this, Ayako Ono examines some of the places Hornel visited during this first trip to Japan in 1893–94. Drawing on

Right. Fig. 20. A Kirkcudbright girl crouching on the edge of a pond, attributed to E. A. Hornel, between *c.*1890 and 1909, glass plate negative

Opposite. Fig. 21. *In the Orchard*, E. A. Hornel, 1898, oil on canvas, image courtesy of City Art Centre, Museums & Galleries Edinburgh

letters, newspaper accounts and a lecture written by Hornel, she introduces the Tokyo that he and Henry experienced. Hornel was fully aware of the dual nature of the modernising country he was in, where the old and the new existed side by side. However, when it came to the photographic material he collected, he was almost solely interested in stereotypical representations of Japan. He collected one particular album of photographic prints during this trip which he immediately amalgamated into his art. Paintings produced in 1894–96 show figures and aesthetics taken from these photographs, even if his painting technique remained essentially Western in character.

Antonia Laurence-Allen then examines in more detail exactly how Hornel worked the Japanese photographs collected on both of his

Above. Fig. 22. Vegetation in Sri Lanka, attributed to E. A. Hornel, 1907, glass plate negative

Opposite top. Fig. 23. *Ceylon Landscape*, E. A. Hornel, *c.*1908, oil on canvas

Opposite bottom. Fig. 24. Bamboo in Sri Lanka, attributed to E. A. Hornel, 1907, glass plate negative

trips into his paintings. She looks at how the photographs provided him with forms to copy as well as a new way of structuring and framing his paintings. While Hornel was fascinated by the poses of the Japanese women in his photographs, he also needed Scottish models to populate his paintings. Laurence-Allen suggests Hornel posed local girls from Kirkcudbright to mimic the gestures of the women captured in his Japanese photographs.

The Japanese photographs that Hornel collected did not just inspire his paintings and his photography in Scotland. They helped him develop a way of working that he would repeat for the rest of his career, no matter what the subject. In 1907, Hornel and his sister Elizabeth visited their cousin James Hornell (1865–1949) in Sri Lanka. While there, Hornel took more than three hundred photographs, mostly of Tamil and Sinhalese women and girls. The poses visible in

many of these photographs would become direct models for later paintings, as well as being repeated in Hornel's own photography in Scotland. His trip to Sri Lanka, the photographs he took there and the subsequent paintings are the subject of Heshani Sothiraj Eddleston's chapter. She delves into some of the nuances visible in Hornel's Sri Lankan photographs, and unpicks the way these subtleties are, or are not, visible in his paintings.

In the following chapter, Ben Reiss and Antonia Laurence-Allen find that Hornel pursued an almost identical approach when he visited Myanmar in 1920, again with Elizabeth. Hornel collected far fewer photographs here than he had in either Japan or Sri Lanka, but he copied them into his paintings in the same direct fashion. Hornel's Myanmar photographs also influenced how he photographed the local Kirkcudbright girls. In a country that was relatively unknown to

Western eyes, he found new and 'exotic' forms to paint, and a foreign world in which to locate his compositions.

Hornel did not just bring back photographs from his travels. He also returned with books, objects and ideas.[13] Like many Westerners who visited Japan, he was influenced and inspired by the aesthetics of the formal gardens that he saw there. Throughout the early years of the twentieth century, he sought to include some elements of what he had seen into his own garden at Broughton House. In this he was not alone, even in Scotland. Jill Raggett looks at this wider trend for Japanese-inspired gardens across Scotland at the turn of the twentieth century, with specific reference to the garden at Broughton House.

The publication finishes with a chapter by Samuel Gallacher on Broughton House itself. Hornel's home from 1900, the house was not just a home and garden; it was also a key location for the production of his art and functioned as a commercial space. Hornel photographed local Kirkcudbright girls and created his paintings in the specially built studio at the back of the house. Gallacher explains how Hornel would move paintings from the studio into the gallery above for display to potential clients. Broughton House also became a home for his extensive collection of books, curios and works of art. After his death in 1933, and that of Elizabeth in 1950, parts of the house were opened up to the public, fulfilling Hornel's wish that it become a public library.

Opposite. Fig. 25. *A Burmese Market*, E. A. Hornel, *c.*1922–27, oil on canvas

Above. Fig. 26. Elizabeth Hornel, Warneuke of Glasgow, undated, photographic print

Broughton House & Garden is now in the care of the National Trust for Scotland, and still contains the furniture and possessions of Hornel and his sister. It holds the artist's approximately seventeen hundred working photographs (as well as hundreds of other more generic prints), along with 74 of his paintings.[14] The exhibition and this publication seek to bring together these two collections and show that each can enrich and illuminate the other. By studying Hornel's photographs, and by holding them up next to his paintings, we can see just how crucial they were to his way of working. This comparison allows for a deeper analysis of Hornel's process, presenting a more rounded view of him as an artist.

GEORGE HENRY
TOKIO

CHAPTER I

HORNEL'S ARTISTIC CONTEXT

Alix Agret

Opposite. Fig. 27. *Japanese Lady with a Fan*, George Henry, 1894, oil on canvas, Glasgow Museums

Above. Fig. 28. A Japanese woman from the back, unidentified photographer, before 1894, photographic print

Hornel's use of photography to aid his painting is far from unique. Other members of the 'Glasgow School' also found in photography a way to sharpen their gaze. Having been apprenticed to a photographer in Glasgow, John Lavery (1856–1941) – an Irish painter associated with the 'Glasgow School' – was well acquainted with the medium and its potential advantages for painters. Naturalist French painter Jules Bastien-Lepage (1848–1884) gave the advice that a subject should be closely observed once (but not twice) and then painted through careful recall. Photography provided the opportunity to observe a subject in the instant, and then to recall it at leisure in the studio. Photography was therefore instrumental in developing the artistic eye at the end of the century.

James Guthrie (1859–1930), also associated with the 'Glasgow School', developed his own method of using photographs. Going out with his camera, he collected details of scenes of landscapes which would then feature in his final work. The sketchbooks of Scottish painter William Kennedy (1859–1918) show evidence that both photography and drawing were important to his painting process. In one of Kennedy's books, for example, photographs of haymakers sit next to preparatory drawings. Stitching together photographic elements to create a painting was something also practised by Hornel.

Similarities between some of George Henry's paintings and Japanese photographs in the Hornel collection suggest that Henry also used photographic models. He borrowed details such as *geisha* hair pins from photographs to showcase Japanese hairstyles. Henry's painting *Japanese Lady with a Fan* (1894, Fig. 27) was very likely inspired by a photograph now in the Hornel collection at Broughton House (Fig. 28). Seen from behind in both the photograph and the painting, the Japanese woman exhibits her neck, considered an erotic zone in Japan. There are still lines visible on the photo which would have aided the act of copying.[1] In *Salutations* (1894, Fig. 29), Henry probably mixed two photographs to create this painting of women greeting. The painted backdrop visible in the photograph and painting prominently features Mount Fuji – a stereotypical image of Japan. Like Hornel, commercial photographs were of primary use to Henry for their female models and exotic clichés. Henry was able to use them to appropriate a remote place and culture in order to give an exotic gloss to his paintings.

Photography was not just known to or used by painters in Scotland. It had always been of interest to Edgar Degas (1834–1917), who was credited as being one of the first artists 'to see what photography could teach the painter', by his friend Paul Valéry.[2] Degas' paintings contain aspects gleaned from photography, such as stiffly posed models in front of flat backgrounds.[3] However, he did not take up photography

Opposite top. Fig. 29. *Salutations*, George Henry, 1894, watercolour, Alamy Stock Photo (original owned by Glasgow Museums)

Opposite middle left. Fig. 30. Jane Morris, posed by Dante Gabriel Rossetti, John Robert Parsons, 1865, albumen print, © Victoria and Albert Museum, London

Opposite middle right. Fig. 31. Jane Morris: study for *Mariana*, Dante Gabriel Rossetti, 1868, chalk on paper, The Metropolitan Museum of Art, gift of Jessie Lemont Trausil, 1947

himself until 1895, when he feverishly began experimenting to 'stretch the accepted procedures and plastic qualities of his materials in photography as he had been in printmaking and pastel'.[4] Degas experimented with photography, trying to photograph the night and integrating accidents like unintended double exposure and solarisation into his images. He took numerous photographs, but very few of them remain.[5] Three glass plate negatives attributed to Degas show a ballerina in various poses, and bear a superficial resemblance to Hornel's photographic images of Japanese and Myanmar dancers. Degas also photographed his friends. He would dictate their poses, which he made them hold for up to 15 minutes at a time, and orchestrated the lighting, in much the same way Hornel directed his sitters in Kirkcudbright to obtain the perfect poses.[6]

In England, Dante Gabriel Rossetti collaborated with John Robert Parsons (1826–1909) to create 18 photographs of embroiderer and model Jane Morris (1839–1914, Fig. 30). These photographs became cornerstones of several of his paintings, including *Reverie* (1868) and *Mariana* (1870; a sketch for the final painting from 1868 can be seen in Fig. 31). Both works are copied almost directly from photographs, and in their emphasis on Morris's hands and features have a decidedly photographic feel.

During the nineteenth century, the camera was considered an objective and scientific instrument which was used to verify and document otherness. Photographs of faraway countries were often used by painters to imbue their work with a veneer of authenticity, whether justified or not. Typical in this respect is the painting *Cairene Horse Dealer* (1867) by French artist Jean-Léon Gérôme (1824–1904), which demonstrates how an appearance of truth can prevail over reality. His Cairene street view is a sample of a stylised Egypt, an invention partly derived from a photograph of Yemenite buildings.

This is the context that Hornel was working in, where painters freely used photographs as compositional aids. However, in his case there is an obsessive feel to the way he accumulated approximately seventeen hundred glass plate negatives and photographic prints from the 1890s to his death in 1933. The majority represent local girls and were taken in Kirkcudbright. However, his collection also comprises photographs from his visits to Japan, Sri Lanka and Myanmar. Interestingly, it was his first Japanese stay that firmly established his interest in the mechanical lens and persuaded him to rely on photography. It is as though he needed to experience cultural distance to allow reproduction and seriality to fully infuse his paintings.

Although Hornel left a huge cache of glass plate negatives, no evidence for his ideas about photography has yet been found in his archive at Broughton House, so we can at best speculate on his theoretical position. While he does not seem to have criticised the mechanisation implied by an automated device, neither did he boast about using it. Perhaps we can then conjecture that he would have aligned himself with the consensus that, as 'an expedient aid toward the completion of the final work of art',[7] photography was but a secondary tool and belonged to the private sphere. Paul Gauguin (1848–1903), for example, ferociously expressed his contempt for what he deemed a technological gizmo: 'Machines have come, art has fled, and I am far from thinking photography can help us.'[8] And yet, he always kept in his pocket a picture-postcard image of Borobudur, a Buddhist temple located in Java, as if its reproduction was a compensation for his disappointing experience of the French colonies, which did not turn out to be the paradise he was expecting.[9]

Hornel started building his own photographic collection in Japan, after spending 13 months in Tokyo and Yokohama, and becoming a member of the Photographic Society of Japan. A large number of the images he collected in Japan in 1893–94 (and during his second visit in 1921) are Yokohama *shashin*, 'typical of the Japanese nineteenth-century photographs that were produced in huge numbers as souvenirs for foreign visitors'.[10] They mainly consist of romanticised depictions of *geisha* presiding over tea ceremonies, dancing or contemplating cherry blossom in gardens. These photos offered the Western eye what it expected to see and revelled in: a sensuous embodiment of an unwesternised Japan, frozen in happy communion with nature and feudal mores untouched by civilisation. Hornel left Scotland hoping to discover exactly this image of Japan, 'a paradise of babies and pretty girls, a land of cherry blossom and seductive tea house life'.[11] He returned with photos that reinforced this ideal, and collected more during his second trip.

With his Japanese photographs, Hornel brought back not just memories to Scotland, but also a method of painting he would keep perfecting over the years. He 'wasn't a natural draughtsman and … he used his camera in place of a sketchbook. It appears that he very rarely executed preliminary sketches.'[12] He relied instead on photography as a painting aid, using the camera to capture almost a thousand images of Scottish girls and young women so he could copy fragments of their bodies into his compositions. His photographs focus on fixing the twist of a head or the pose of a hand, foot or arm. This suggests that Hornel's priority was to gather these fragments of the body with photography before using oil painting as a way to compose the perfect whole.

By working in this way, his models were reduced to patterns which he appropriated and refashioned ad infinitum. Hornel effectively created a pattern book of poses and contortions, with hundreds of subtle variations of crouching, crawling, sitting, standing or lying bodies documenting a standardised anatomy. Apart from their simple dresses, the girls that sat for Hornel are anonymised, deprived of any distinctive social signs or class signifiers. They are removed from their

Fig. 32. A Japanese woman in a *kimono* with a flowering plant, unidentified photographer, before 1921, Yokohama *shashin* print

Right. Fig. 33. The hands of a Kirkcudbright girl, attributed to E. A. Hornel, between 1909 and 1933, glass plate negative

Middle. Fig. 34. The bare feet of a Kirkcudbright girl, attributed to E. A. Hornel, between 1909 and 1933, glass plate negative

Bottom. Fig. 35. A Kirkcudbright girl in a black skirt crawling, attributed to E. A. Hornel, between 1909 and 1933, glass plate negative

Opposite top. Fig. 36. The head and shoulders of a Kirkcudbright girl lying on a rug, attributed to E. A. Hornel, between 1909 and 1933, glass plate negative

Opposite bottom. Fig. 37. Three Kirkcudbright girls lying on the grass, attributed to E. A. Hornel, between c.1890 and 1909, glass plate negative

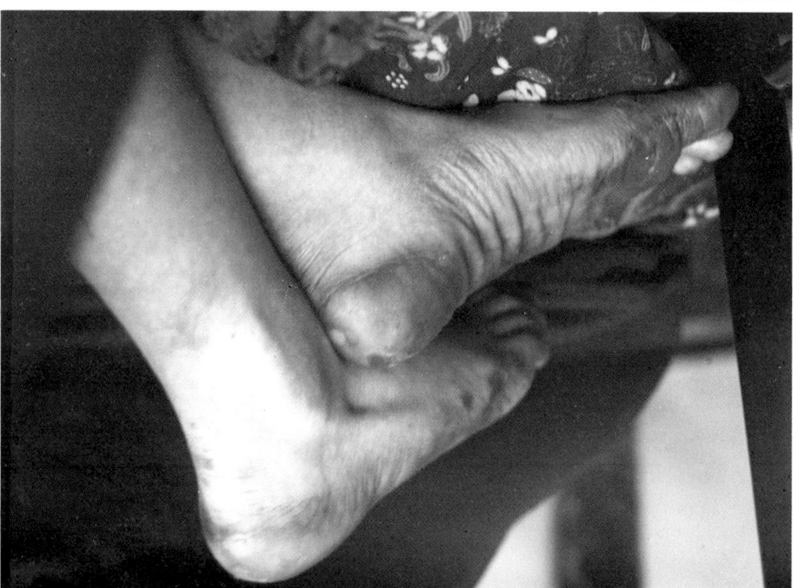

Above left. Fig. 38. Hornel posing a Kirkcudbright girl in a black dress outside, attributed to Robert McConchie, between c.1890 and 1909, glass plate negative

Above right. Fig. 39. Hornel turning the head of a Kirkcudbright girl in a black dress outside, attributed to Robert McConchie, between c.1890 and 1909, glass plate negative

cultural and historical context since their background – predominately the painter's studio – is unchanging and unconnected with their lives.

Just occasionally, reality disrupts the meticulous arrangements planned by Hornel. In one photograph (Fig. 36), a gap in the model's front teeth and stains on her dress betray her individuality, contradicting Hornel's ornamental uniformity. She 'escapes' the pose, resisting his visual construction. It is as if she were returning his gaze and questioning him, her magnetic stare now haunting our own vision of his paintings.

Hornel himself can be seen intruding into several photographs, directing a child's pose or watching attentively. This underlines the key function of these studio sessions; specifically, that they were carefully choreographed to capture what he had already visualised. However, repeated photos of girls prostrating themselves for Hornel, and images of him manipulating their bodies into the required pose, point to attitudes which might be uncomfortable for a modern viewer.[13]

The legal definition of childhood was the subject of much debate during the Victorian era, with the age of feminine sexual consent in Great Britain being raised from 12 to 13 in 1875, and to 16 in 1885. Childhood was understood as an extended period of sexual latency and it was believed that children's relative closeness to God spared them from sin. It was usual for 'sexless bodies of naked tykes [to adorn] postcards and salon paintings alike, their forms appearing not as a sexual invitation but rather an emblem of incorruptibility'.[14]

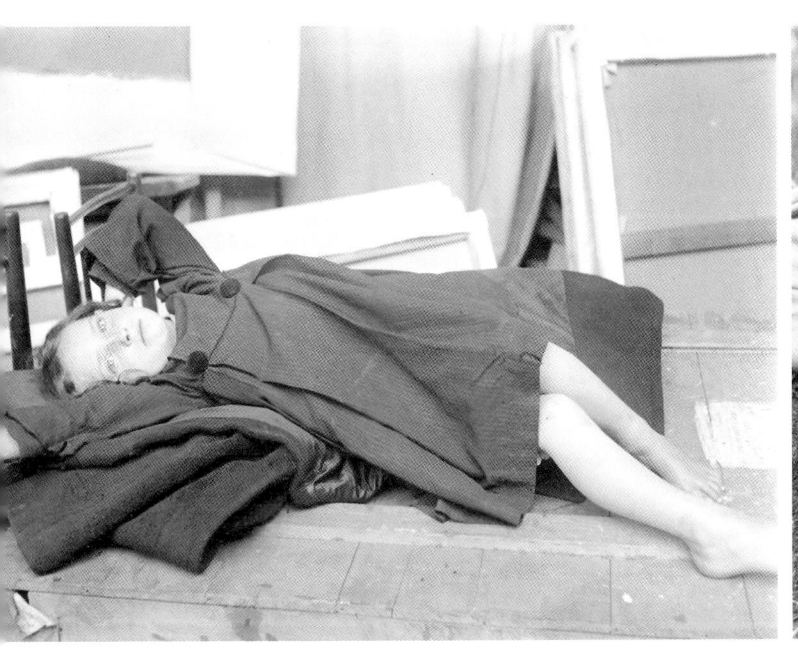

Above left. Fig. 40. A Kirkcudbright girl in a black dress lying on a rug, attributed to E. A. Hornel, between 1909 and 1933, glass plate negative

Above right. Fig. 41. Two Kirkcudbright girls lying on the grass, attributed to E. A. Hornel, between *c.*1890 and 1909, glass plate negative

In Hornel's paintings, the girls conform to this asexuality, their existence limited to a blissful immersion in nature. They are forever giving themselves up to flowers and placid expanses of water. But these works are replete with what they deny, confirming that 'the more it was disavowed, the greater the presence of sexuality as the central feature of bourgeois life' became in the nineteenth century.[15] Neither Hornel's paintings nor his photographs need to contain nakedness for sensuality to creep in; *The Toy Boat, Brighouse Bay* (1925, Fig. 42) is a rare example of Hornel painting nudity. Full of repeated images of girls sprawled on couches and interlocking limbs, there is a sense of eroticism in Hornel's photographic collection, particularly to the modern eye.

In this, Hornel's photographs bear comparison with pictures of children by Lewis Carroll (1832–1898) or Julia Margaret Cameron (1815–1879). Commenting on the undercurrent of eroticism in Cameron's photographs representing the figure of the Madonna, Anne Marsh argues that the series is really one 'of the most subversive presentations of sexuality … in the disguise of religious reverie'.[16] Skin against skin, child and mother are interlocked in incestuous embraces, signalling Cameron's actively voyeuristic gaze. Hornel's Scottish photographs lack a similar subversive edge, as adults are not pictured, but the images still share much of the visual language of Cameron and Carroll.

To say that Hornel's photographs conform to contemporary attitudes to childhood and sexuality, which we now find uncomfortable, is not to judge him by modern standards, nor is it to suggest for a

Fig. 42. *The Toy Boat, Brighouse Bay*, E. A. Hornel, 1925, oil on canvas

moment that anything untoward occurred at the Broughton House studio. The girls were brought to Hornel by their mothers, chaperoned by Hornel's sister Elizabeth, and were paid for their time. To pose for Hornel seems to have been considered an honour by the models, even if today we might question their ability to give meaningful consent in a modern sense.[17]

Hornel's photographic treatment of children is in marked opposition to the thematically similar autochromes produced by photographer John Cimon Warburg (1867–1931) in the early twentieth century. His intimate portraits are imbued with a feeling of preciousness and uniqueness, often intensified by colour. In Warburg's photographs, an individualised girl seen reading a book, standing in a garden or dressed up is captured in dreamlike plays of light, personifying the sophistication of her upper-class life. The key reason for this difference is that while Hornel was photographing anonymous girls to build up an archive of poses, Warburg was creating portraits of individuals – his daughters.

Nor are Hornel's photographs 'enquiries into the beauty or spiri-

Above left. Fig. 43. Alice Liddell as 'The Beggar Maid', Lewis Carroll, 1858, albumen print, The Metropolitan Museum of Art, New York, Gilman Collection, gift of The Howard Gilman Foundation, 2005

Above right. Fig. 44. *The Madonna Penserosa*, Julia Margaret Cameron, 1864, albumen print, The Metropolitan Museum of Art, New York, Harris Brisbane Dick Fund, 1941

tuality of the models' like Cameron's, whose images apparently glorified the uniqueness of children.[18] Hornel's photos do nothing to ennoble children or photography, unlike Cameron, whose soft focus, references to literature, imitation of Renaissance art and adherence to Pre-Raphaelite ideals were being used to legitimise photography as an artistic form. Hornel's photography also had nothing to do with a quest for realism or an alternative vision of the world. He did not collect photographs to accurately record Japanese, Sri Lankan, Scottish or Myanmar life, nor did he seek to glorify a muse or loved one. His photographs of girls and young women were intended as purely functional resources.

Hornel's focus on youth as a subject matter conformed to a conception of childhood that originated from British eighteenth-century philosophical views on the nature and rights of mankind. Romanticised, the child was no longer considered an imperfect grown-up, rather an embodiment of innocence whose redemptive contact benefited adults.[19] Art championed this cult of childhood and attempted to preserve in paint or stone the transience of youth. By

Fig. 45. *Mine Own Back Garden*, E. A. Hornel, 1887, oil on canvas, © The Hunterian, University of Glasgow

the end of the nineteenth century, the Romantic child – the personification of unspoiled humanity – had become a cultural artefact. This commodification is epitomised by *Cherry Ripe* (1879) and *Bubbles* (1886), the two portraits by John Everett Millais (1829–1896) which were used in Pears soap advertising. The reassuring sentimentality such images conveyed was popular in an age of growing industrialisation, and evoked 'the possibility of restoring England to its "old-fashioned" Edenic state'.[20] Hornel, too, would seek to take advantage of a nostalgic yearning for 'old-fashioned' Britain with his own pastoral paintings of girls surrounded by green foliage and blossom.

In their desire to 'record contemporary life in a natural manner', the painters of the 'Glasgow School' theoretically rebelled against

Fig. 46. *A Cottar's Garden*, George Henry, 1885, watercolour on paper

what were considered the treacly excesses of the 'glue pot' art of artists like Millais.[21] These Scottish artists advocated realism and *plein-air* painting, mainly focusing on contemporary rural scenes. Hornel's *Mine Own Back Garden* (1887, Fig. 45) and Henry's *A Cottar's Garden* (1885, Fig. 46) encapsulate a factual and dispassionate approach, almost photographic in their treatment of the 'real'. However, this concern with the physical appearance of people, inherited from French naturalism, gave way to a more decorative style of painting as the artists became less interested in depicting the socio-economic conditions of their models. By the early 1890s, Hornel and Henry were producing paintings such as *The Druids: Bringing in the Mistletoe* (Hornel and Henry, 1890, Fig. 47) and *Summer* (Hornel, 1891, Fig. 77), where design

Fig. 47. *The Druids: Bringing in the Mistletoe*, E. A. Hornel and George Henry, 1890, oil on canvas, Glasgow Museums

prevails over representation. The children of *Summer* are not realistically painted, but instead are incorporated in an arrangement of colours and shapes that blends figures and background.

This merging of girls and nature, something that became increasingly exaggerated in Hornel's work, may well have been inspired by paintings such as *Le Père Jacques* (1882) by Naturalist painter Bastien-Lepage. *Le Père Jacques* is a prime example of how Naturalist painters 'identified the focus of the camera lens as the most modern way of viewing a subject. Imitating the eye of a camera, they would focus on

Above left. Fig. 48. *Girls Resting by the Irrawaddy*, E. A. Hornel, *c.*1922–27, oil on canvas

Above right. Fig. 49. A Kirkcudbright girl sitting on a cushion with Elizabeth visible behind, attributed to E. A. Hornel, between 1909 and 1933, glass plate negative

certain details such as a person's face or foreground foliage, while surrounding areas would appear slightly blurred or out of focus.'[22]

This description encapsulates Hornel's approach to painting from the late 1890s onwards. Photographic sharpness dissolves in the haziness of his thick impasto backgrounds. Except for faces and limbs – which are the 'photographic' focus – the girls fade into the landscape, sometimes to the point of melting into abstraction. In these paintings, the bodies of the girls almost disappear, in stark contrast with the Realist treatment of Hornel's early paintings and his photographs, which depict figures clearly delineated against their setting. He idealises his subjects to the point where a corporeal reality ceases to be a requirement.

This way of working may have allowed Hornel to distance himself from his models and treat the girls as objectified shapes rather than

Above. Fig. 50. *Brighouse Bay, Wild and Burnet Roses*, E. A. Hornel, 1929, oil on canvas

Opposite. Fig. 51. Two Japanese women with fans, E. A. Hornel, *c.*1921–30, oil on canvas

people, thus erasing the need to add any social, economic or geographic specificity.[23] He uses poses and compositions interchangeably, creating an indeterminate space in his paintings where he could take advantage of the popular fashion for imagery of childhood. Although the titles of the paintings might refer to 'Burma' or 'Brighouse Bay', and the country of origin of the girls might change, Hornel's treatment of his models does not. Whether from Japan, Scotland, Sri Lanka or Myanmar, they float in front of the same thick impasto backdrop; a floral continuity incorporates Kirkcudbright, Japan and the British colonies in the same idyllic land, obliterating differences. In Hornel's paintings, it is as if nothing changes from one continent to another except for the vegetation and the skin colour of his models.

CHAPTER 2

A WESTERN GAZE ON AN EASTERN SHORE

Jennifer Melville

Opposite left. Fig. 52. *Two Geishas*, E. A. Hornel, 1894, oil on canvas

Opposite right. Fig. 53. *Courtesan (after Eisen)*, Vincent van Gogh, 1887, oil on cotton, Van Gogh Museum, Amsterdam (Vincent van Gogh Foundation)

The visit that George Henry and Hornel made to Japan over 1893–94 is seen as a crucial time in their development as artists. For both men it must have remained a salient time in their careers. However, for Hornel, his highly developed understanding of Japanese art and aesthetics did not initially result from going to Japan but instead first came about through his close connection with modern art in Europe, where several artists were changing the way that they painted, in a direct response to their exposure to Japanese art.

As a young man, through the winter of 1884 and most of 1885, Hornel studied at the Royal Academy of Fine Arts in Antwerp, under Charles Verlat (1824–1890). Verlat became the Academy's director in 1885 and it was Verlat whom Vincent van Gogh (1853–1890) sought out when he arrived in Antwerp in late November that year.[1] Van Gogh wanted Verlat to comment on his work and teach him life drawing, but it was the city itself that gave him real inspiration. This was a critical point in van Gogh's career: it was the moment when he recognised how Japanese art made him see the world around him in a completely different way. As he explained to his brother: 'My dear Theo, ... a few more impressions of Antwerp ... these docks are one huge Japonaiserie, fantastic, singular, strange ... colourful and bustling ... so tangled that one can find no rest for the eye, so that one gets dizzy ... by the flickering of colours and lines'.[2]

Van Gogh decorated his Antwerp studio with Japanese prints of 'little female figures in gardens or on the shore, horsemen, flowers, gnarled thorn branches'[3] and began to echo the forms, pattern and colour of Japanese prints in his own paintings. A craze for all things Japanese was sweeping across Europe, and *ukiyo-e* woodblock prints were core to this craze. Van Gogh, and some of his contemporaries, began to emulate the bright colours and unfamiliar compositional devices found in these prints, which included a steepened perspective and objects and figures cut off at the edges. This cutting-off was due to the fact that the prints were often originally shown together as a diptych or triptych, with one composition running through the set. All such elements were to become vital components of what became known as Post-Impressionism.

Van Gogh returned to Paris in 1886 and lived with his brother Theo and the Glasgow art dealer Alexander Reid (1854–1928).[4] Upon returning to Scotland, Reid staged an exhibition of prints by Katsushika Hokusai (1760–1849) – one of Japan's best-known printmakers – in Glasgow in 1889 and became Hornel's supporter and dealer. Reid recognised how Hornel had embraced the most dynamic, Japanese-inspired aspects of Post-Impressionism. Significantly, just before leaving for Japan in February 1893, Hornel exhibited with Les XX, a progressive

Fig. 54. *The Goatherd*, E. A. Hornel, 1889, oil on canvas, Glasgow Museums

Belgian art group, which he had been aware of since his time in Antwerp.[5] Each year Les XX invited a few international artists to exhibit with them. They included Camille Pissarro (1894), Claude Monet (1840–1926), Georges Seurat (1859–1891), Paul Gauguin (1848–1903), Paul Cézanne (1839–1906) and van Gogh.[6] Les XX accepted four works by Hornel, including *The Goatherd* (1889, Fig. 54) and *The Brook* (1891, Fig. 55), both of which show a clear debt to Japanese print

Fig. 55. *The Brook*, E. A. Hornel, 1891, oil on canvas, © The Hunterian, University of Glasgow

compositions but also reveal a marked change in Hornel's art between the dates of their creation, that is between 1889 and 1891.

In 1889, Hornel had introduced the steep and flattened perspective of Japanese prints into *The Goatherd*. However, by 1891, when he painted *The Brook*, he was alone amongst his Scottish contemporaries in his use of thick impasto, overall decorative patterning and intense colour –

Fig. 56. *The Olive Trees*, Vincent van Gogh, 1889, oil on canvas, Museum of Modern Art, New York, Mrs John Hay Whitney bequest

elements which van Gogh had recently pioneered. Shared motifs appear too: the gnarled tree trunk in *The Brook* is a distinctive feature of Japanese *ukiyo-e* woodcut prints and one that fascinated van Gogh. He painted no fewer than 15 pictures of such trees, first in 1887 when he made a copy of Utagawa Hiroshige's (1797–1858) *Plum Park in Kameido* (1857), then developing the theme in his own compositions.

Van Gogh knew that visiting Japan would be impossible – Provence, with its sunshine and colour, would have to serve as a stand-in. For Hornel and Henry, however, experiencing Japan was to become a reality. *The Brook* had been bought by the wealthy shipping merchant William Burrell (1861–1958) and he, along with Reid, agreed to fund the trip, on the understanding that it would result in a body of Japanese-inspired work that would hopefully benefit them all.

Hornel and Henry arrived in Japan on 21 April 1893 and at first were disappointed to discover that the Japanese did not normally dress in the elaborate traditional costume that they had anticipated. Writing to a friend, Henry explained: 'At home one gets a mistaken idea as to the dress of the Japs. Really they dress very plain and in very quiet colour'.[7]

Indeed the 'floating world' conjured up in *ukiyo-e* prints was an exotic one, full of bright colours, dramatic action and exciting opportunities. There was no division between art and what some might view as pornography in Japanese art. Sexually explicit *shunga* or erotic 'spring pictures'[8] were included in the numerous prints circulated and collected in Europe, most notably by the French critic Edmond de Goncourt (1822–1896). These erotic prints must have suggested that modern-day Japan would be not just physically, but also metaphorically, a world away from Presbyterian Scotland, with its sombrely dressed citizens and a sexual underworld that remained largely hidden from polite society, although not necessarily from young Glasgow artists like Henry.[9] In Japan, Henry and Hornel may have hoped that they would find the opportunity to transcend social boundaries and experience an entirely different life.

They arrived at a time when Japan was tentatively opening to the West. The very few British people there were bringing tangible benefits to Japan, in fields like engineering, shipping and seismology. These were educated men who admired and respected the Japanese people, seeing parallels in their own colonial desire to expand and at the same time remain aloof from the rest of the world.

Unlike in the British colonies, where marriage with the indigenous population was unusual and seen only amongst lower-class expatriates (ordinary soldiers in India, for example), in Japan it was not uncommon. Several of Henry and Hornel's acquaintances, including the eminent seismologist John Milne[10] (1850–1913) and the Scottish engineer William Kinnimond Burton[11] (1856–1899), married Japanese women. Indeed, Burton wed Orakawa Matsu[12] during Hornel and Henry's stay, on 19 May 1894, at a ceremony at the British Consulate in Tokyo.

Henry's revealing letter came at the start of their sojourn, when he seemed unable to understand modern-day Japan. He made few meaningful connections[13] and had no love for the Japanese people: 'Upon my soul the people here don't seem human beings somehow'.[14]

Hornel (albeit on his return to Scotland the following year) delighted in the clever ways in which Japanese rooms could be subdivided by screens and how spotlessly clean everything was. He found Japanese dancing 'strange', 'sedate and beautiful' and extolled their perfect manners, their love of nature and their 'raising of the commonplace into the region of art, and investing it with charm at once the despair and envy of the European'.[15]

However, although Hornel rejected the prejudices and racial stereotyping of previous authors, his own terminology is troubling: the population as a whole are 'Japs' or 'little creatures', the rickshaw drivers 'coolies'. Still imagining himself to be in the floating world of *ukiyo-e*, he focuses only on the idyll that he has decided to depict:

> It is disagreeable, indeed almost impossible for me, to associate the Japanese with politics and their consequences … rather do I associate and love to remember them, as a large and happy family, clattering along in the sunshine, with smiling faces and no thought of the morrow, to spend the day 'mid plum or cherry blossom, or at night joyous and elevated with saki, amusing themselves with pretty geishas, dancing to the weird music of the samisen.[16]

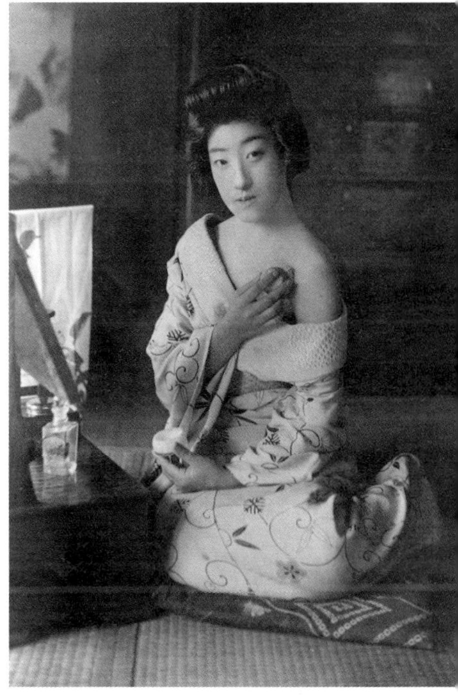

Fig. 57. A Japanese woman with bare shoulders, unidentified photographer, probably 1893–94 or 1921, photographic print

In describing only this idyll and ignoring all other elements of this fast-changing society, he in effect infantilises the Japanese people. In his memory, like children they seem to live only for the moment and have no concerns or care for the future.

Despite this dreamy account of his stay in Japan, the reality was quite different. Henry discovered that Yoshiwara, the red-light district of Tokyo, might offer a solution to the apparent lack of exoticism: 'the only exception in the way of gay colour such as we always picture them, are the frail beauties of the Yoshiwara'.[17] Yet, the 'frail beauties' proved difficult to access:

> the Yoshiwara girls sit in cages displaying their charms to the passer by on the street. They never appear abroad, at least very seldom, and never with their clothes except for a religious procession, and nobody here seems to have ever seen one, as the police just allow them to have one if they choose.[18]

To Henry's chagrin, however, strict controls were enforced on foreigners over what might be described as sex tourism today. Hornel found a way round this, and not just so that he could access girls wearing traditional costume, as Henry revealed: 'Phallicism is still rampant in many places so Hornel is happy. He is down at a fishing village just now called Misaki. I believe it is one huge brothel'.[19]

It is disconcerting for a modern viewer to look through the hundreds of photographs that Hornel brought back from his time in Japan. These images capture, in the main, very young women and girls, some acting out tasks but many simply posing, often looking coyly at the camera and in some cases partially undressed. *Geisha* were prohibited from engaging in prostitution but it is thought that the majority did so, as did many girls who were below the legal age for prostitution, which was 18.[20] Whether due to his sexual proclivities, or merely his preferred subject matter, Hornel's choice of sitters suggests that he was particularly drawn to the young. He was not alone; it has been much debated whether there was something sinister about Lewis Carroll's fixation with six-year-old Alice Liddell (1852–1934, Fig. 43), or that of J. M. Barrie (1860–1937) with Michael Llewelyn Davies (1900–1921), the boy on whom Peter Pan was based. In fact throughout the Victorian period there was a degree of acceptance of what now seem unhealthy obsessions and inappropriate depictions of children. This is also seen in earlier Scottish art, as in *The Arrochar Gleaner* (1862, Fig. 58), a fanciful depiction by Robert Herdman (1829–1888) of a gleaner which, like Carroll's photograph of Alice Liddell, combines discomforting eye contact with a provocative off-the-shoulder ragged dress.

On his return to Scotland, Henry was planning to have slides made up (perhaps for a talk) of the most salacious aspects of their lives in Japan. He wrote to Hornel: 'My Dear Ned, Could you send up the Photos of the Girls in the Bath and if you have them one or two of exterior of the Y[oshiwara] showing the cages system. I want to get Annan to turn these into slides. G.H.'[21] For Hornel the photographs remained a private study collection. Although he used his photographs as a basis for his compositions – and may even have projected the images onto the canvas – he was very careful to tone down the overt sexuality of his young sitters when adding them to his painted compositions. Hornel only hinted at the burgeoning sexuality of these pubescent girls with the titles of numerous subsequent pictures, which reference the awakening or coming of spring and the picking of various springtime flowers.

The numerous photographs that Hornel took and collected whilst in Japan were to prove a continuing inspiration to his work, but they remain by far the most problematic element of his work. Only in his

Fig. 58. *The Arrochar Gleaner*, Robert Herdman, 1862, oil on canvas, Aberdeen Art Gallery and Museums (Aberdeen City Council)

private hoard of photographs, taken or collected in Japan, can we see past the public persona that Hornel projected: the creator of numerous anodyne Japanese paintings, in which children laugh, sing, play music, fly kites and go fishing. Only in the photographs, which were never exhibited, do we get a glimpse of a particular aspect of Japan that Hornel witnessed and experienced. This is not the Japan of brightly dressed, gay and innocent girls, but instead the unpalatable reality of pubescent prostitutes earning a living in a patriarchal society, all viewed with a questionable and unnerving Western male gaze.

CHAPTER 3

ENCOUNTERS WITH MODERN JAPAN

Luke Gartlan

Opposite. Fig. 59. Three Japanese women in *kimono*, unidentified photographer, before 1921, Yokohama *shashin* print

George Henry and Hornel's arrival in Japan coincided with a period of tremendous activity in the photographic circles of Yokohama and Tokyo. With the assistance of the Camera Club in London, the Photographic Society of Japan (Nihon Shashinkai) was in the final stages of organising an *Exhibition of Foreign Photographs*. This watershed exhibition, which opened in Ueno Park, Tokyo, on 13 May 1893, brought around three hundred works by some of the most significant British photographers of the nineteenth century – including such luminaries as Julia Margaret Cameron (1815–1879) and Peter Henry Emerson (1856–1936) – before the appreciative public of the Japanese capital. The exhibition brought to Japan works by photographers associated with the Linked Ring, which had been established the previous year to promote the tenets of pictorialism in British photography.[1]

Having disembarked at Yokohama in the weeks preceding the opening of this exhibition, Henry and Hornel quickly became involved in its preparations. At a meeting of the Photographic Society of Japan on 20 May, the work of the two visiting artists was formally acknowledged 'to whose untiring energy for several days was due the excellent way in which the photographs were hung'.[2] This curatorial role was an important aspect of the exhibition, given its broader aim of promoting the artistic credentials of photography in Japan. Henry and Hornel were unanimously elected members at the same meeting of the Photographic Society, formalising their association and providing direct access to its influential membership. Examining the two artists' associations with local photographers and painters in Japan highlights their debt to these professional networks.

From their very first days in Japan, Henry and Hornel were directly involved in the local photography scene and introduced to its key figures. Their involvement in the Photographic Society brought them into contact with the leading photographers and cultural luminaries of the country. The press report of the society meeting indicated that the two artists, in response to the praise bestowed on them for the exhibition display, pandered to the audience assembled before them:

> Mr. Hornell [*sic*], in replying, said that, speaking as an artist, he considered the work of Japanese photographers quite up to that shown at the present Exhibition. He said some very bitter things about the Exhibition of Oil Paintings being held next door to that of the photography, as also did Mr. Henry.[3]

In order to provide the means for audiences to assess this judgement, a display of Japanese photographs by members of the society supplemented the foreign exhibition, inviting direct comparison between the two bodies of work. As a related report announced in the *Japan Weekly Mail*, the Japanese photographs 'will be viewed with special interest in consideration of the opinion expressed … by one so capable to give judgment as Mr. E. A. Hornell [*sic*] concerning the comparative artistic merits of the works of Japanese and foreign photographs'.[4]

For the expatriate readership of this English-language Yokohama newspaper, Hornel performed the role of visiting expert who brought the cachet of metropolitan approval to domestic photography in Japan. The comparative merit bestowed on their work was consistent with the increasing international attention and confidence that had resulted in the establishment of the Photographic Society of Japan in 1889. Its membership included a surprisingly diverse and influential group of Japanese and non-Japanese advocates of photography, including leading politicians, chemists, industrialists, aristocratic enthusiasts and *ukiyo-e* artists. The society expanded rapidly with regular meetings, competitions, lectures and excursions, all of which were reported in its own monthly journal, *Shashin Shinpō* (*Photographic News*). Hornel's positive assessment thus confirmed the high self-esteem of the photographic circles of Japan, evident in their display of their own work beside their foreign counterparts.

Henry and Hornel's high regard for Japanese photographers stands in stark contrast to their out-of-hand dismissal of an adjacent exhibition of Japanese oil painting in Ueno Park, about which they expressed some 'very bitter things'. Beyond this brief reference cited above the report had no more to add, but this adjacent exhibition of the Meiji Fine Arts Society (Meiji Bijutsukai) included some of the leading Japanese artists of Western-style oil painting (*yōga*). The short shrift afforded this exhibition was consistent with the general animosity toward the practice of painting in a Western style in Japan as nationalist sentiments led to the promotion of so-called Japanese-style painting (*nihonga*). For Henry and Hornel, the reasons for their negative appraisal of the exhibition may well have reflected their own rejection of the tenets of academic-style oil painting, but this animosity was also strengthened by their own expectations of Japanese society. In an interview back home in Glasgow, Henry acknowledged that they had 'mixed a good deal among the native artists there', but that these artists 'are foolishly adopting the tricks of Paris and Munich'.[5] While the Japanese artists with whom they mixed are not mentioned by name, the circumstantial evidence suggests that they most probably included such artists as Yamamoto Hōsui (1850–1906), Goseda Yoshimatsu (1855–1915) and Harada Naojirō (1863–1899). These artists had returned from training in Paris (Yamomoto and Goseda) and Munich (Harada) in the late 1880s and, with others, established the Meiji Fine Arts Society in order to promote Western-style oil painting in Japan.

In the late nineteenth century, numerous British artists travelled to Japan in search of aesthetic and cultural inspiration for their own practice. For many British artists and tourists, the work of these Western-style oil painters was anathema to the search for Japanese cultural authenticity. Such animosity did not extend, however, to their attitudes towards Japanese photography. Both oil painting and photography were foreign imports to Japan, but Henry and Hornel's divergent responses to these adjacent exhibitions highlight the differences in the cultural stakes that had adhered to each media. Yet despite this difference in critical response, the two adjacent exhibitions in Ueno Park emphasise the level of interdependence of the two nations' artistic currents and societies. British and Japanese photographers and painters were in closer dialogue than ever before and the resulting cultural and visual exchanges were multiple, overlapping and ongoing. Accordingly, an art historical approach is required that remains conscious of medium-specific debates and responses across cultural boundaries, but embraces the transcultural and intermedial practices and debates between late nineteenth-century Britain and Japan. Henry and Hornel's engagement with photography during their visit to Tokyo is representative of these wider cultural associations, but their lack of serious engagement with the oil paintings of the Meiji Fine Arts Society represented a lost opportunity to engage with their Japanese counterparts.

Henry and Hornel's collecting practice also highlights the Victorian-era distinction in attitudes towards photography and oil painting in Japan. Whereas European and American visitors to Japan collected photographs in vast numbers, supporting the rise of a burgeoning domestic photographic industry, very few visitors are known to have acquired Western-style oil paintings from Japanese artists. In this respect, Henry and Hornel are no exception. They avoided Western-style oil painting but purchased about 140 photographs during their 13-month visit to Japan, now preserved at Broughton House. Most of these photographs were acquired from the largely export-based souvenir photographers in Yokohama. From the 1860s, Yokohama was the major centre for export commercial photography in Japan, catering primarily to the influx of globetrotters who arrived at the port en route around the world and purchased photographs as souvenirs of their visit. By the time Henry and Hornel arrived in Japan, a small number of Japanese-managed studios dominated the souvenir photography market in Yokohama.

Henry and Hornel's photographic acquisitions are largely consistent with that of other foreign male tourists to Japan of the period. For example, the photograph of three seated women before a painted backdrop, surrounded by chrysanthemums and carefully arranged to display their hairstyles and dress, typifies the photographic propagation of the 'beautiful woman' or *bijin* trope in late nineteenth-century Japanese visual culture (Fig. 59). Young women feature prominently in Henry and Hornel's photographic collection, indicative of the sexual politics that informed their acquisitions in Japan. Many remain difficult to attribute to specific studios, but at least 30 hand-coloured costume photographs (e.g. Fig. 3), inscribed 'by Tamamura, Kobe, Japan', derive from the renowned photographer Tamamura Kōzaburō (1856–*c.*1923), whose main studio in Yokohama had immense success in catering to foreign customers.

Yet while the Glaswegian artists may well have encountered such work in Yokohama, Tamamura was also a prominent contributor to the Japanese section of the photography exhibition at Ueno Park. He was a key connection between the Photographic Society of Japan, whose members largely consisted of amateur enthusiasts and prominent advocates, and the fiercely competitive commercial world of Yokohama souvenir photography. Tamamura had joined the Photographic Society in 1889 soon after its foundation and made a significant contribution to the Japanese section of the photography exhibition.[6] In a review in the *Japan Weekly Mail* of the exhibition at Ueno Park, the anonymous correspondent singled out the hand-coloured contributions of the Yokohama-based studios of Tamamura and Tonokura Tsunetarō (active 1886–1904) for particular attention:

> At all events we have never seen any English coloured photographs that could hold their own against the pictures sent to this Uyeno [Ueno Park] display by Messrs. Tamamura and Tonokura of Yokohama, for example. The former's exhibits are especially remarkable. Their photographic character is entirely effaced, and one's sense of colour and delicate execution is wholly captivated by their exquisite tones and wonderful clearness and softness.[7]

Overall the reviewer remained unconvinced of the merits of Japanese photography in comparison to the British contributions, but admitted that the hand colouring of Yokohama photographs was unrivalled. Such a position had long been established as a defining feature of Yokohama souvenir photographs. It comes as no surprise, particularly given their public statement on the merits of Japanese photography, that Henry and Hornel acquired a large portfolio from Tamamura and other undocumented studios in the Yokohama-Tokyo area. The following month the *Photographic Times* in New York reprinted this review in full, highlighting the international interest in the exhibition and the rising prominence of Japanese photographers.[8]

If Henry and Hornel became aware of the work of Japanese contemporary photographers and painters during their stay, this was in no small part due to the assistance of expatriate residents who had made Japan their home and often served as local advisors and intermediaries for foreign visitors. As Scottish artists on tour in Japan, Henry and Hornel benefited from the expatriate communities and networks in Japan and their close relations with Japanese officials and cultural figures. Although source evidence is circumstantial, the Scottish engineer William Kinnimond Burton certainly assisted Henry and Hornel during their visit to Japan. Burton was a co-founder and driving force behind the Photographic Society of Japan as well as a prolific author and editor on photographic matters. He was the principal figure responsible for organising the exhibition in Ueno Park in collaboration with the London Camera Club and the author of several deluxe photographic publications in association with Japanese photographers such as Kajima Seibei (1866–1924) and Ogawa Kazumasa (1860–1929). Despite periodic bouts of illness, Burton was an energetic advocate of photography and demonstrated a talent for building bridges between diverse individuals irrespective of cultural or social background. Henry and Hornel undoubtedly profited from his pragmatic counsel and extensive local contacts.

The Irish-born Captain Francis Brinkley (1841–1912), then editor of the *Japan Weekly Mail*, was also an important local advisor to the Scottish artists in Japan.[9] In this instance, Henry and Hornel arrived in Japan ready prepared with a letter of introduction for the local editor.[10] Brinkley was another of those extraordinary long-term residents of Japan with diverse interests in Japanese culture and the local business and political connections to match. As the various columns in the *Japan Weekly Mail* suggest, Brinkley took an active interest in the promotion of the photography exhibition at Ueno Park and the domestic arts in general. In fact, Brinkley may confidently be credited with the authorship of the press reports cited above that refer to Henry and Hornel's pursuits in Japan.

Despite the fragmentary sources, Brinkley appears to have remained engaged with Henry and Hornel throughout their 13-month stay in Japan. Only a fortnight before the two artists' departure from Japan on their homeward voyage, Brinkley published another article on 5 May 1894 in the *Japan Weekly Mail*. Taking a review of Henry and Hornel's work from the London *Art Journal* as the pretext for a response, Brinkley provided a lengthy preamble that demonstrates his awareness of the artistic debates that pertained to the 'Glasgow School' and its contributions to contemporary painting in Europe:

> We are weary of the photographic landscapes, the common-place portraits of common-place people, and the cheaply sentimental anecdote pictures that year after year hang on the Academy walls, just as weary as we are of those Ibsen's [*sic*] and Zola's [*sic*] of the palette who in France and Munich and elsewhere strive to obtain immortality for what is ugly, coarse, and material beyond all description. So that in these days of sore decline it must assuredly be considered a sign of better times that a school of Impressionists like the Glasgow School should be gradually and surely winning its way into favour; in other words, that it is becoming understood. Impressionism does not signify to its own represetatives [*sic*] an impersonal record of visual impression: it signifies rather a style for the expression of their individual conception of nature and for the manifestation of personal feeling. And the first canon of their artistic faith is that decoration shall be the basis of picture-making, wherefore they follow in the footsteps of the great prophet and master of modern Impressionists, Whistler. It is not our concern here to inquire of them concerning the truth of the faith they hold. The two members of the group whose work has been seized upon as representative of the general principles of the school, Messrs. Henry and Hornel, have been for some time in Japan, so that it may be interesting to note what the critic has to say of their canvases.[11]

A reprint of the *Art Journal* column then follows, which primarily concerned Henry's and Hornel's work prior to their arrival in Japan. Brinkley's initial comments, however, are significant in bringing these metropolitan debates to English-reading audiences in Japan. The passage includes one of the earliest references published in Japan to James Abbott McNeill Whistler (1834–1903), 'the great prophet and master of modern Impressionists', and places Henry and Hornel at the forefront of contemporary artistic currents in Europe. Brinkley's attempt to distinguish their practice from 'what is ugly, coarse, and material beyond all description' might well be considered overstated, but these comments nonetheless highlight the awareness of European contemporary painting debates and practices in Japan. Such views might well have been informed not only second-hand through art journals and exhibition reviews from abroad, but also through direct contact with visiting artists such as Henry and Hornel as well as Japanese artists and intellectuals on their return from abroad. Whatever the imagined cultural and geographical distance that sustained Orientalist tropes of Japan, Brinkley asserts the increasing exchange and translation of ideas, materials, artists, and media between the art worlds of late nineteenth-century Europe and Japan.

Opposite. Fig. 60. Two Japanese women posing with fans in a studio, possibly E. A. Hornel, probably 1921, glass plate negative

In conclusion to this review, Brinkley returned to the local context to report on the two artists' activities over the previous year:

> Contrary to the usual habit with artists visiting Japan, neither of these gentlemen, we believe, has completely finished any single picture during his stay here. They have rather busied themselves with the amassing of material and the laying in of ground work, which can more easily be worked up at home than in Japan, and we look forward with no little eagerness to the results of their visit. It is our opinion that people at home will be invited to look upon a new and more than usually fascinating interpretation of the land of the Rising Sun.[12]

Given Brinkley's personal association with Henry and Hornel and close engagement with the local arts scene, the suggestion that the two painters had completed little during their year in Japan is feasible. In this respect, the large number of photographs acquired during their visit might well have constituted the mass 'of material and the laying in of ground work' that had constituted their activities in Japan. In addition to the hand-coloured export photographs, the Hornel collection at Broughton House also includes several glass plate negatives of Japanese women and children in performance (Fig. 60). With their lack of colours, direct lighting, basic studio setting, and exceptional rarity, these plates may have been either specially commissioned or were the result of Henry and Hornel's own efforts with a camera in Japan. Hornel had already experimented with photography in the years before his departure for Japan, and Henry's and Hornel's membership of the Photographic Society of Japan would have provided access to the requisite materials and inspiration during their extended sojourn. Whatever the case may be, Henry and Hornel's photograph collection furnished the raw visual materials for selective use in the oil paintings of Japanese subjects completed on their return home in the summer of 1894.

Henry and Hornel were indebted to photography and painting networks in Japan that aided and informed their own engagement with the country through which they travelled. Far from isolated painters in pursuit of fanciful subjects, they were the beneficiaries of the transcultural networks that had brought Japanese and British photographers and artists into close dialogue and interaction over the previous four decades. Henry's and Hornel's use of photography highlights the necessity for a visual history that examines diverse media and practices not in isolation from one another, but as interconnected and integral to the local and global visual currents and practices that bound late nineteenth-century Scotland and Japan.

694. UYENO TOKIO

CHAPTER 4

HORNEL'S VISIT TO JAPAN (1893–94) AND HIS USE OF PHOTOGRAPHY

Ayako Ono

Opposite. Fig. 61. '694: Uyeno Tokio', Kusakabe Kimbei, between 1881 and 1894, albumen print

Japanese art had a great impact on Western artists in the late nineteenth and early twentieth centuries in Europe. Many British artists, including Christopher Dresser (1834–1904), Alfred East (1844–1913) and Mortimer Menpes (1855–1938), travelled to Japan to explore Japanese life and culture for the creation of their art. Hornel and his friend George Henry were two such Scottish artists who visited Japan from 1893 to 1894, with expectations that an experience of an unknown world might improve their success as painters. When Hornel and Henry travelled east, it was with a 'desire to see and study the environment ... to become personally in touch with the people, to live their life, and discover the source of their inspiration'.[1]

Many of the photographs Hornel collected in Japan are typical Yokohama *shashin*. Some were taken by Tamamura Kōzaburō, who opened his studio in Yokohama in 1882, while others are photographs of women in *carte de visite* size, which were sold very cheaply in the Ueno (Fig. 61) and Asakusa (Fig. 63) districts of Tokyo. In addition to these, the Hornel collection includes an album with a simple thick wooden cover which contains photographs taken in Egypt and Japan.

Known documentary records of Hornel and Henry's visit are limited. They include five short letters from Henry to Hornel written in Japan,[2] an interview which Henry gave to the local newspaper, *Castle Douglas*, soon after their return in 1894,[3] and Hornel's public lecture, presented – at the invitation of James Paton (1843–1921) – at the Corporation Art Galleries in Glasgow on 9 February 1895.[4] Paton was a curator who had arranged the exchange of gifts between Glasgow and the Meiji government in 1878 and 1879. Although the lecture was delivered by Hornel's friend, the architect John Keppie (1862–1945), it was prepared by Hornel.[5]

In 1893, Hornel and Henry sailed to Japan from Liverpool. Their arrival in Nagasaki on 21 April was reported by the *Glasgow Evening News*.[6] In the interview with *Castle Douglas*, Henry said that they were based in the Concession in Tokyo. This was Tsukiji-teppōzu (Fig. 62), an area established in 1869 for foreign residents in the very centre of Tokyo, which was formerly known as Daimyo Yashiki, the residential area for feudal lords. The area is located along the riverfront of the Sumida River and was ideally suited for segregating foreigners.

The Tsukiji settlement was not as large as the concessions in Yokohama, and many of the residents were consular officials and missionaries who had established schools in the area. It seems that Hornel and Henry received substantial support from British residents in Japan. For example, in October 1893, Henry wrote a letter to Hornel saying 'Parlett's camera is not quick enough for this',[7] and also on 6 October 1893, Henry concluded a letter to Hornel with: 'with love from Parlett

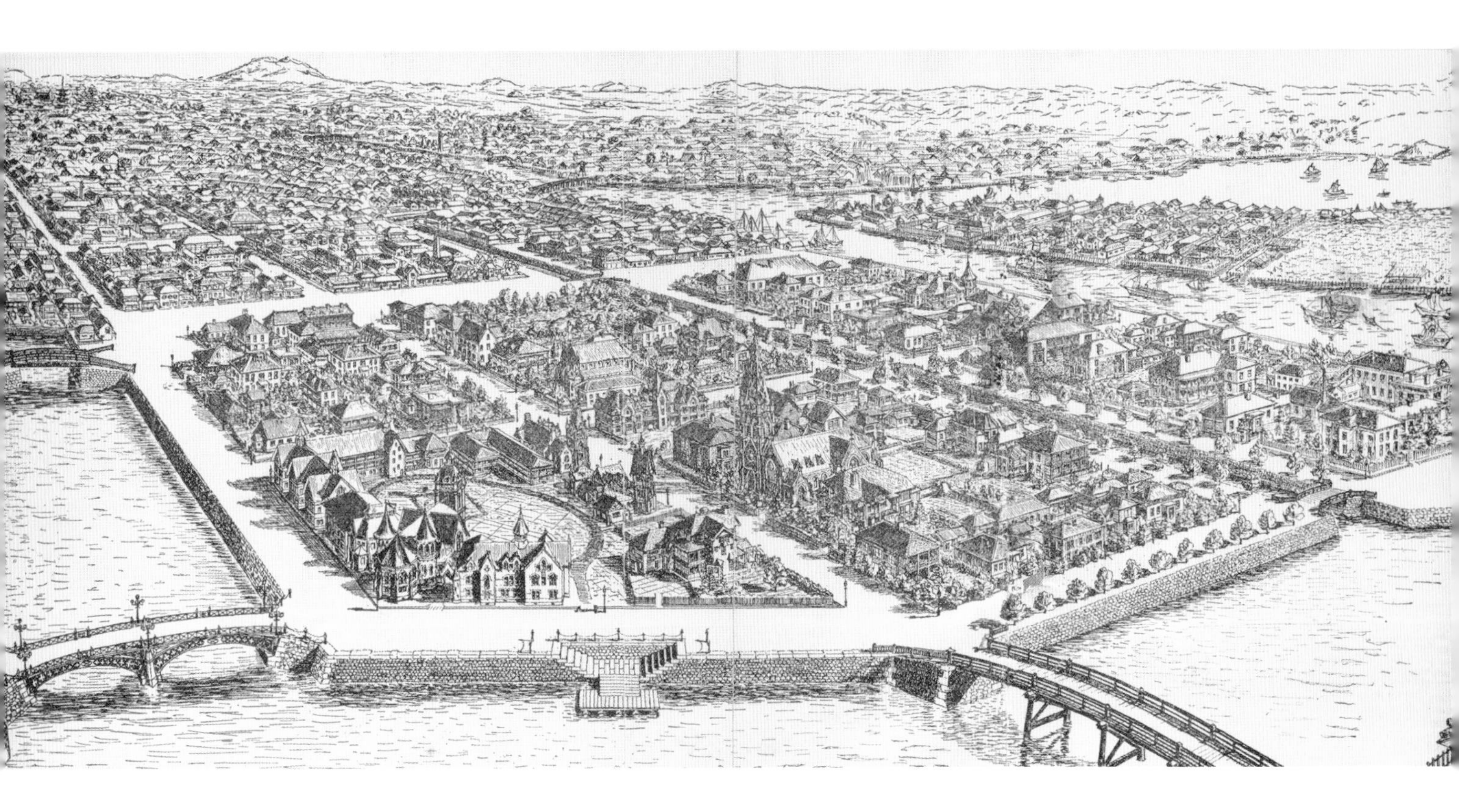

Fig. 62. The Tsukiji-teppōzu area of Tokyo, J.M. Gardiner, 1894, etching, Rikkyo University Library, Rikkyo Archives, Tokyo

and "Yoroku" [Yoroshiku] to the household'.[8] Harold George Parlett (1869–1945) was a student interpreter who went to Japan in 1890 and successively held diplomatic posts until his retirement in 1927. He was chairman of the Photographic Society of Japan,[9] published works on Buddhism and the Japanese language[10] and was knighted in 1924.

Although the precise location of Hornel's residency cannot be confirmed, a letter from Captain Francis Brinkley to Hornel confirms that he did frequent the Tsukiji area. Brinkley wrote, 'I have been twice to look for you. Once I called at the Hotel Metropole, & subsequently I went to search for you in company with Mr. Curtis, but we failed to find your house.'[11] The Hotel Metropole building was originally the US legation; it was transformed in 1890 into a branch hotel of The Club Hotel Ltd, Yokohama, after the legation moved from Tsukiji to Akasaka. In 1893, it was renamed after the Hotel Metropole on Whitehall Place in London, because this UK hotel hosted the annual meeting of the Japan Society.[12]

Tsukiji was a place where Hornel likely saw a mixture of old and new Japan, as the country transitioned from the Edo period to the Meiji period. Despite this, he almost exclusively collected photographs that catered to a foreigner's stereotypical idea of Japan, generally avoiding anything that might have appeared too Western. Tsukiji is within

Fig. 63. '708: The great high building at Asakusa, Tokio' – the Ryōunkaku skyscraper, unidentified photographer, between 1890 and 1894, albumen print

walking distance of the Imperial House and Henry reported that he and Hornel had once seen the Meiji Emperor:

> The Mikado. Oh! all right. We got a glimpse of him one day, and he struck us as being the ugliest person it had ever been our privilege to clap eyes on. He wore a sort of European uniform, and indeed the Court and society have adopted European ideas to the extent of making our store clothes take the place of their own beautiful and artistic costumes.[13]

The negative reaction of Hornel and Henry to seeing the Meiji Emperor in 'European ... store clothes' rather than Japanese 'beautiful and artistic costumes' reinforces the idea that the two artists were primarily interested in the stereotypes they had come to Japan to find.

Tsukiji was also the neighbourhood of Shintomi-cho, where the first modern *kabuki* theatre was located, a photograph of which is included in the Hornel collection at Broughton House. In the Edo

Fig. 64. Shintomi-za, the main *kabuki* theatre in the Tsukiji-teppōzu area of Tokyo after rebuilding, unidentified photographer, 1885, albumen print

period, *kabuki* was considered lower-class entertainment and theatres were located in Saruwaka, in the Asakusa district. However, after the Meiji Restoration, *kabuki* actor Morita Kanya (1846–1897) modernised Japanese theatre. In 1872, he built the first modern *kabuki* theatre in Shintomi-cho, an elite Tsukiji area open to foreign residents. This theatre, Morita-za, was renamed Shintomi-za (Fig. 64) in 1875. A year later it was destroyed by fire, but it was soon rebuilt as a modern Westernised building with gas lights and chairs. The reopening of the theatre in 1878 was celebrated with Western-style music played by the army and navy, and invited guests dressed in Western clothing.

Hornel experienced this changing Japan while he was in and around Tsukiji, but he also explored life beyond the foreign settlement. Ueno and Asakusa are about four miles from Tsukiji. In his 1895 lecture, Hornel described 'the *jinrikisha* (man with a hand cart) [as] indispensable' and reported that 'Taking one of these to go to Ueno Park, you pass through most of the principal thoroughfares of Tokio [*sic*]'.[14] Taking *jinrikisha* to go to Ueno and Asakusa, Hornel must have

Fig. 65. Modern-day *geisha* in the Asakusa area of Tokyo with the Kaminarimon (Thunder Gate) reflected behind her, Saruwatari Haruko, 4 November 2017, digital photograph, Sunnydays in Tokyo

enjoyed a little sightseeing of Kyobashi, Nihonbashi and the Sumida River, areas that are well known from *ukiyo-e* prints.

In his 1895 lecture, Hornel also explained the history of Ueno Park. It was a popular place, as Hornel said, especially as a cherry blossom viewing spot. It was not only 'the most popular resort'[15] but also the cultural and educational area of Japan's first national museum, the Tokyo National Museum, whose main building was designed by the British architect Josiah Conder (1852–1920) in 1881.

Asakusa was, in Hornel's time (and remains today), a popular entertainment area in Tokyo. Hornel himself noted:

> the grounds of Asakusa are the quaintest and liveliest place in Tokio. Here are raree shows [peep shows], penny gaffs, performing monkeys, cheap photographs, street artists, jugglers, wrestlers, life size figures in clay, vendors of toys and lolly-pops of every sort, and circulating amidst all these cheap attractions, a seething crowd of busy holiday makers.[16]

In addition, Asakusa was known for its large red-light district – Yoshiwara – which included *geisha* entertainment. Although the size of the district is now much smaller, the world of *geisha* still exists there today (Fig. 65). It is clear that Hornel sometimes spent his evenings in Asakusa and enjoyed watching *geisha* dancing. He said in his lecture, 'once you have started, the mistress of the house, knowing you cannot live by bread alone, enquires which particular Geisha you wish to call in'.[17] While Hornel's experience of *ozashiki-asobi* (*geisha* entertainment in a traditional Japanese restaurant or tea house) was almost certainly an inspiration for his paintings of Japanese subjects, the specific female forms and compositional elements that appear in them are to be found in his photographic collection.

While the use of photography is significant in Hornel's art, especially in his paintings of Japanese subjects, to start with he did not simply copy the figures and compositions of the photographs. In most cases, he chose one or two figures as a main motif, then added other figures and an interior or exterior setting. He generally did not use his photographs to guide the way he painted the backgrounds of his painting. For instance, when Hornel painted *The Fish Pool* (1894, Fig. 66), he used a photograph from his wood-covered album, in which five children are looking at a book (Fig. 67).[18] He took two children from this photograph but added a different background to the painting, inserting a woman wearing a *kimono* and a Japanese lantern. Although one of the girls is holding a book in the photograph, in the painting she holds a bamboo fishing pole. Unlike the children in the

Fig. 66. *The Fish Pool*, E. A. Hornel, 1894, oil on canvas, Glasgow Museums

Fig. 67. Five Japanese children reading beneath blossom, unidentified photographer, before 1894, albumen print

Above. Fig. 68. *Japanese Dancing Girls*, E. A. Hornel, 1894, oil on canvas, Alamy Stock Photo, private collection

Right. Fig. 69. '22: Dancing Party', Kusakabe Kimbei, between 1881 and 1894, albumen print

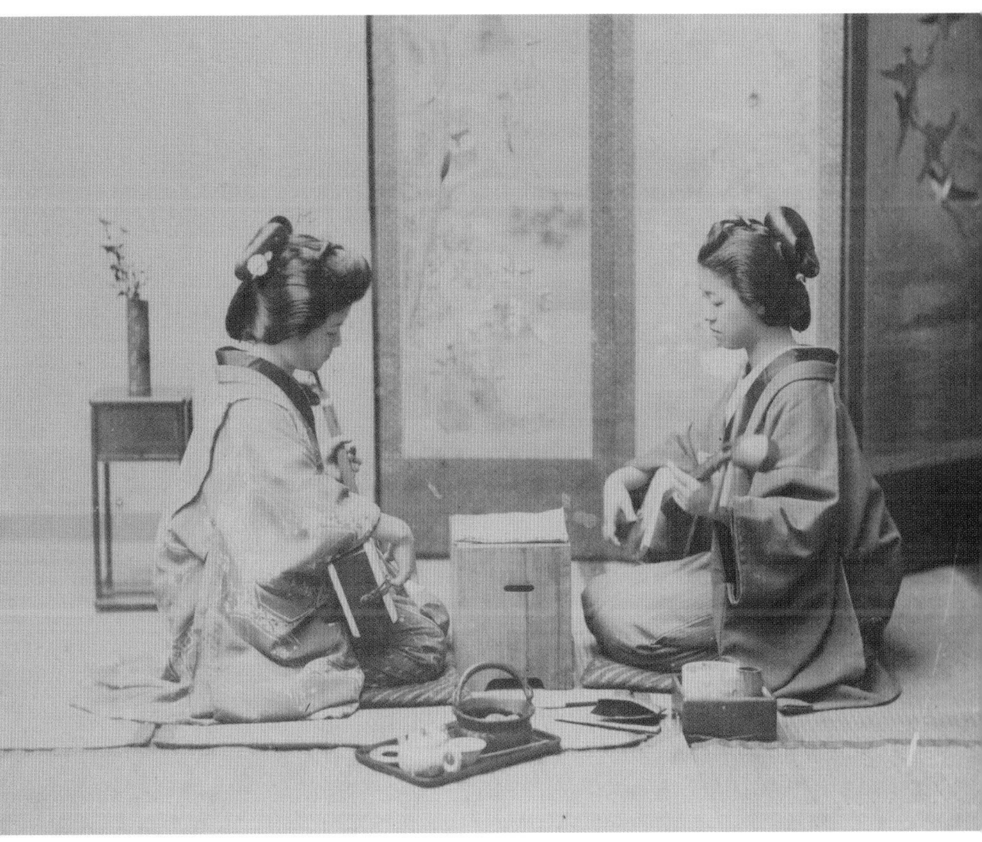

Above left. Fig. 70. '1533: Playing at Tsuzumi', unidentified photographer, before 1894, albumen print

Above right. Fig. 71. Two Japanese musicians, unidentified photographer, before 1894, albumen print

photograph, those in Hornel's painting are lively and smiling. In addition, Hornel changed the *kimono* patterns from simple stripes to colourful designs, and has given the children hair ornaments. Hornel used and adjusted the photograph he brought back to Scotland to create an easily recognisable and commercially viable vision of Japan.

Hornel often used multiple photographs as inspiration for a single painting. For instance, he used five photographs, both loose prints and some from his wood-covered album, for *Japanese Dancing Girls* (1894, Fig. 68). He took dancing women, musicians and musical instruments from a variety of photographs (Figs 69–71), and arranged them as a merry party like those he may have enjoyed in Asakusa.

For his painting *Figures with Lanterns and a Bridge* (1894, Fig. 72), Hornel used at least two photographs. One of these can be identified as Kameido Tenjin Shrine from the wisteria trellis and arched bridge (Fig. 73). The shrine is (and would have been) very well known thanks to prints produced by Hokusai in 1834 and Hiroshige in 1856. It was therefore a suitable subject for an artist seeking an immediately recognisable image of Japan. The other photograph is of the back of a single female figure (Fig. 28). The surface of this photograph reveals lines

Above left. Fig. 72. *Figures with Lanterns and a Bridge*, E. A. Hornel, 1894, oil on canvas, © The Hunterian, University of Glasgow

Above right. Fig. 73. Kameido Tenjin Shrine, unidentified photographer, before 1894, albumen print

that Hornel drew to transfer the image directly onto his painting, although in the painting he has also added a Japanese umbrella, as if the woman was avoiding sunlight. The composition and background of this photograph are simple. Unlike the commercial images in the wood-covered album, it is possible that it (as well as the photograph of Kameido Tenjin Shrine, which is also not in the album) was taken by Hornel himself or his friends in Japan, possibly through the Photographic Society of Japan.

Another photograph (Fig. 75) with a simple composition, plain background and lines drawn on the surface shows a woman playing the *koto* (Japanese harp). Her pose and the pattern of her *kimono* were copied directly by Hornel when he painted *The Duet* (1896, Fig. 74). However, as was usual for Hornel, he chose to change the background, painting her outside surrounded by blossom instead of inside. Hornel seems to have understood some aspects of the Japanese custom of flower viewing. He wrote: 'This reverence for everything in nature, finds its truest expression in their [Japanese people's] passion for flowers, especially those of the cherry, and gives us an insight into their true character.'[19] A photograph of blossom in Ueno Park in the wood-covered album gives an idea of what Hornel's own experience of flower viewing there might have been like (Fig. 61). The influence

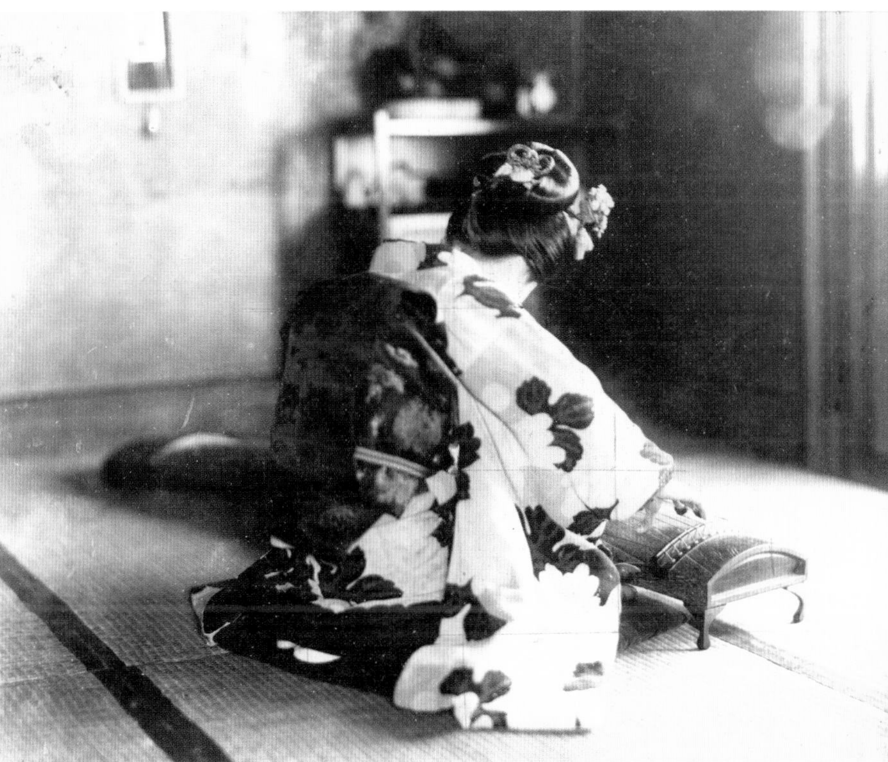

Above left. Fig. 74. *The Duet*, E. A. Hornel, 1896, oil on canvas, private collection

Above right. Fig. 75. A Japanese woman playing the *koto*, unidentified photographer, before 1894, albumen print

of this experience is visible in the floral background of *The Duet*.

As a foreign resident in Japan in the late nineteenth century, Hornel witnessed a country in transition. His interactions in Tsukiji, Ueno and Asakusa provided him with new subject matter to paint. His 13-month stay allowed him to observe annual events and traditional games like *hanetsuki* (battledore and shuttlecock) and *takoage* (kite flying), that were often played at New Year, and which subsequently appeared in his paintings. Hornel visited places famous for specific species of flowers, which he would also later paint, such as Ueno for cherry blossoms and lotus flowers and Kameido Tenjin for wisteria. In his 1895 lecture, Hornel showed his attitude was to keep a distance from modern politics and remember his experience of 'smiling faces', 'plum or cherry bloom', 'amusing themselves with pretty geishas' and 'dancing to the weird music of the samisen [*shamisen*]'.[20]

During his stay, Hornel collected photographs of Japanese people, especially women and children, and of Japanese scenery. Many of these images were both widely exported and also provided as souvenirs in Japan for foreign visitors in the late nineteenth century. However, Hornel used them in his own way and, in the decorative quality of his paintings inspired by these photographs, expressed the liveliness of his encounter with Japan.

CHAPTER 5

HORNEL AND JAPAN: DEVELOPING A PHOTOGRAPHIC EYE

Antonia Laurence-Allen

Opposite. Detail from Fig. 78. A Japanese woman in a *kimono* (note the paint and pin marks), unidentified photographer, before 1921, Yokohama *shashin* print

The photographic material in the Hornel collection at Broughton House (especially elements collected during trips to Japan, Sri Lanka and Myanmar) has been largely unexplored. Recent reappraisal has led to a new understanding of Hornel's painting process. Hornel and George Henry set off for Japan in 1893 with a desire to experience an 'authentic' Japanese way of life for themselves. Whether Hornel did indeed experience authentic Japan is up for debate, but he certainly brought home a greater understanding of how to use the camera.

Hornel had been taking photographs before he went to Japan. There is a glass plate negative that captures a young girl with hobnailed boots, sitting on the grass grinning widely (Fig. 76); she is the same figure seen in Hornel's 1891 painting *Summer* (Fig. 77). As noted by Alix Agret in Chapter 1, Hornel was aware that fellow painters in Scotland, like John Lavery, E. A. Taylor (1874–1951) and James Paterson (1854–1932), were also using photographs to aid their work.[1] Therefore, it is no surprise that he and Henry joined the Photographic Society of Japan when they arrived in Yokohama. The society had many foreign amateur photographers, including William Kinnimond Burton who had been hired under the Meiji initiative[2] to teach civil engineering at the Tokyo Imperial University in the late 1880s. Burton and the commercial photographer Ogawa Kazumasa[3] were founding members of the society. Inaugurated in 1889, the Photographic Society of Japan was Japan's first organisation for amateur photographers; 24 of the 56 founding members were foreigners. As such, the society was a social network for outsiders who wished to truly 'experience'

Right. Fig. 76. A Kirkcudbright girl holding a hat, attributed to E. A. Hornel, *c.*1890, glass plate negative

Opposite. Fig. 77. *Summer*, E. A. Hornel, 1891, oil on canvas, Walker Art Gallery, National Museums Liverpool

Fig. 78. A Japanese woman in a *kimono* (note the paint and pin marks), unidentified photographer, before 1921, Yokohama *shashin* print

Japanese life. Just before Hornel and Henry arrived in 1893, Ogawa had produced photographs for an exhibition called *100 Beauties*. These were studied portraits of Tokyo's *geisha*. This display was commissioned to mark the opening of Japan's first skyscraper (the Ryōunkaku, Fig. 63) in 1891. It was a publicity stunt, designed to encourage visitors to climb the tower and vote for the most beautiful woman. The Ryōunkaku was designed by Ogawa's photographic colleague Burton.

Luke Gartlan has noted in Chapter 3 the extent to which joining the Photographic Society of Japan helped Henry and Hornel to meet local photographers and established foreigners, as well as gain access to theatres, exhibitions and modelling sessions. Members went to local theatres and tea houses to watch dancers perform. They were also given the chance to capture women posing in the privacy of a studio setting and wearing *kimono*. In 1893 – and when he went again in 1920–21 – Hornel seems to have taken advantage of the activities and modelling sessions organised by the society. At Broughton House there are many glass plate negatives of Japanese girls and women, all focusing on specific actions and expressions. Hornel was fascinated by the gestures and movement of Japanese dance, which he said was 'made up of quaint posturing, dignified and refined movements, with delicate and artistic and pretty manipulations of the fan'.[4]

As a rapidly developing technology, the camera was very much part of the modern world, and Japanese photographers recorded infrastructure projects, building works and contemporary life (including the Meiji Emperor depicted in modern dress).[5] Concurrently, studios started catering to Western markets and fed audiences with the well-established image of Japan as 'a land of quaintly beautiful women and flowers and fans and sunshades'.[6] Yokohama *shashin* were highly valued for their colours, detail and design, and focused on Japanese tradition, costume and feudal customs. Women were photographed in studios with backdrops or out among the cherry blossom, wearing patterned *kimono*. In these images, their arms are often raised to show off the distinctive wide sleeves of the *kimono* or their bodies are twisted to ensure a glimpse of the *obi* knot at the back. Heads tilt forward or gently to the side to highlight the complexity of the hairstyle, whilst the hands and feet are set in arched and graceful ways that would have been considered peculiarly 'exotic' by Western viewers.

The photographs in Hornel's collection can be roughly divided into three sets. First, the commercial Yokohama *shashin* prints, which feature stylised women, interiors and landscape scenes (Figs 78 and 79). These gave Hornel a set of static, formulaic poses, depicting women and girls performing a tea ceremony or standing in a Japanese

Fig. 79. Two Japanese women in *kimono* greeting each other (note the paint and pin marks), unidentified photographer, before 1921, Yokohama *shashin* print

Fig. 80. Three Japanese women in an interior, E. A. Hornel, *c.*1921–25, oil on canvas

garden. Many of these were taken by Photographic Society of Japan members known to Hornel, including Ogawa and Tamamura Kōzaburō, and reinforced the 'ideal' Japanese woman as a submissive figure divorced from modernity; a trope echoed by European photographers like the Venice-born Felice Beato (1832–1909), who was based in Yokohama in the 1860s.[7] These photographs were clearly vital to Hornel's work; many have been jabbed through with pins or splashed with paint as he used them for reference while he worked in his studio.

The second type of image in Hornel's Japanese collection is the result of studio modelling sessions, presumably organised by the Photographic Society of Japan (Fig. 60). These may have been taken by Hornel (or Henry), but may have been taken by another photographer, as he was sent images of two Japanese women when he returned to Japan in 1921.[8] The glass plate negatives capture women and girls posing informally in a basic studio setting with ubiquitous and highly incongruous matting and backdrop. Their bodies are more languid than the static figures in the hand-coloured Yokohama *shashin*. In what seems like an effort to extend the poses found in commercial photography, these studio photographs provide the expression and dynamism that had captivated Hornel when he attended the dance halls and theatres.

Fig. 81. Two Japanese women wearing *kimono*, unidentified photographer, probably 1893–94 or 1921, photographic print

Finally, the third set of images capture women in informal poses, almost exclusively outside (Fig. 81). It is not clear if these were taken by members of the Photographic Society of Japan for private use or whether they were available commercially. In these photographs – almost snapshots – groups of girls laugh with one another, and single women engage with the camera in a confident manner. The women are posed with an ease that is not evident in the formal Yokohama *shashin* and seem more spontaneous than the studio shots.

After his return to Scotland in 1894, Hornel honed an approach to painting that always seemed to begin with a photographic image. His first exhibition of paintings, in 1895 at Alexander Reid's gallery in Glasgow, was a commercial and critical success (he sold nearly all of the 40 works on display).[9] One critic declared it 'one of the most magnificent displays of a single artist's genius ever brought together in Scotland'.[10] Another suggested that no other artist who had visited 'the land of the cherry' had 'returned with a more comprehensive pictorial record of Japanese life'.[11] It was not necessarily modern life in Japan that Hornel 'comprehensively' recorded in his paintings, but the feudal past. It was Japanese tradition that was capturing the imaginations of consumers in Glasgow and across Western Europe, thus Hornel gave audiences what they desired. Added to this was the popular subject matter of girls and young women, caught – out of

time – in some idyllic pastoral scene. The paintings Hornel produced on his return from Japan mimicked the vertical format seen in many of the Yokohama *shashin* prints he collected. These compositions take elements from a variety of photographs. Some images gave him the tilt of the head; others the vivacious designs on the *kimono* or the flutter of a fan. Hornel's colour palette became richer, and the use of black to outline costumes and bodies became more pronounced. This can be clearly seen in his 1894 painting *Two Geishas* (Fig. 52), where Hornel may have used a variety of photographs as reference (see, for example, Figs 61, 82 and 83).

While Hornel had started to experiment with a Post-Impressionist vivacity of colour and brushstroke before his visit to Japan in 1893, his foray into the exoticised world of the imaginary East helped him

Above left. Fig. 82. '*Geisha* girls out for an airing. These young ladies form a portion of the stock-in-trade of the tea house in view', Tamamura Kōzaburō, probably between 1883 and *c.*1900, Yokohama *shashin* print

Above right. Fig. 83. 'A Singing Girl', Kusakabe Kimbei, between 1881 and 1894, albumen print

Fig. 84. *Harvesting, Kirkcudbright*, E. A. Hornel, 1885, oil on canvas

to move away completely from the muddied, dull, tones seen in his earlier Scottish landscape paintings.

From the late 1890s, Hornel perfected his painting technique; the backgrounds become more abstract and the hands and faces of his figures are thrown into sharper focus. All this was done in conjunction with his increased interest in using photographs in his painting process and an attempt to recreate a rural idyll in his own backyard. To do this, Hornel required Scottish faces. In the years following his initial trip to Japan, he produced over one thousand glass plate negatives, capturing local Kirkcudbright girls that would then feature in his painting compositions. Many of these photographs focus on the sitters' hands, faces and feet, and replicate poses found in the Japanese prints.

Hornel purchased Broughton House in September 1900 and, shortly afterwards, made plans to add a large studio and gallery; his

Left. Fig. 85. *Young Girl with Primroses*, E. A. Hornel, 1906, oil on canvas

Above. Fig. 86. A Kirkcudbright girl wearing a white bonnet, attributed to E. A. Hornel, probably *c.*1906, glass plate negative

Below left. Fig. 87. A Japanese girl dancing with a fan in a studio, possibly E. A. Hornel, probably 1893–94 or 1921, glass plate negative

Below middle. Fig. 88. A Kirkcudbright girl posing with an easel, assisted by Elizabeth, attributed to E. A. Hornel, *c.*1906–10, glass plate negative

Below right. Fig. 89. A Kirkcudbright girl holding on to an easel in the studio at Broughton House, attributed to E. A. Hornel, *c.*1906–10, glass plate negative

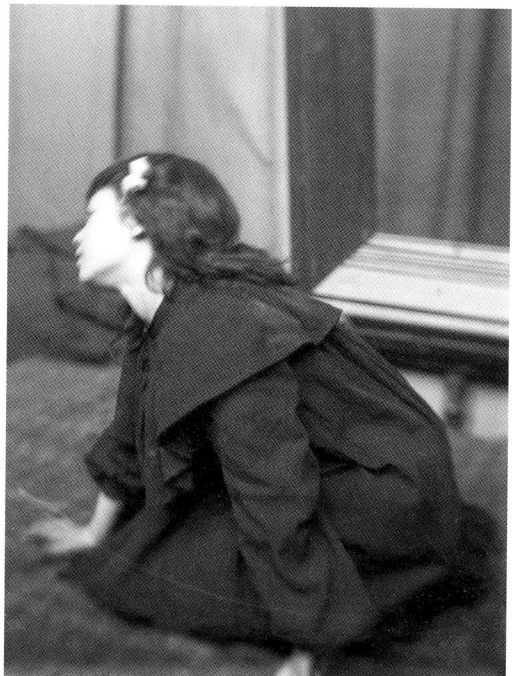

Above left. Fig. 90. Two Japanese women dancing in a studio, possibly E. A. Hornel, probably 1921, glass plate negative

Above right. Fig. 91. A Kirkcudbright girl in a black dress facing away from the camera, attributed to E. A. Hornel, *c.*1906–7, glass plate negative

Right. Fig. 92. A Kirkcudbright girl posing with her hand to her chin, attributed to E. A. Hornel, *c.*1906–07, glass plate negative

sister Elizabeth became his housekeeper. Local girls, brought by their mothers and chaperoned in the studio by Elizabeth, began posing for Hornel's camera. A friend, Robert McConchie, helped with the photography and Hornel directed the girls. He got them to move in ways that reflected the distinctive poses and hand gestures of the Japanese dancers. The girls ranged in age, between roughly seven and 17, and came from a variety of local families.[12] Hornel was a local

Fig. 93. *Seashore Roses*, E. A. Hornel, c.1907, oil on canvas, image courtesy of City Art Centre, Museums & Galleries Edinburgh

landlord and played a large role in Kirkcudbright politics and cultural life. Under these conditions, the power relationship (as we would call it now) was overwhelmingly balanced in his favour, as mothers and their girls would have had little choice but to acquiesce to this rather unconventional arrangement. However, there is no suggestion the arrangement was anything other than unconventional. His models felt privileged to pose for him and, as a public figure, there would have been plenty of attention on both Hornel and his home.

All these photographs of Kirkcudbright girls became a valuable resource for Hornel. It is clear he used the images to compose the perfect painting. He took a hand from one photograph, a tilt of the head from another and the curve of a back from a third, then filled the background with the suggestion of nature. It is not the identity

Top left. Fig. 94. Two Japanese girls holding baskets in a studio, possibly E. A. Hornel, probably 1921, glass plate negative

Above left.: Fig. 95. Two Japanese girls posing with baskets in a studio, possibly E. A. Hornel, probably 1921, glass plate negative

Above right. Fig. 96. *Three Japanese Peasants*, E. A. Hornel, 1921–25, oil on canvas

of an individual he sought to interpret but the ideal surface of the female form; a purely objective exercise to find the ideal pose. Indeed, in some instances, he reused the same individual in different poses within one painting, indicating that it was form, not individuality, that Hornel sought to capture.

Hornel's collection of photographs shows the girls rooted in the reality of the studio; nervous sometimes, often joyful. Yet in paint that sense of glee or naiveté is surrounded by an increasingly frenzied and thick impasto; the suggestion of a tree, or a flowering shrub, hints at a world far removed from any modern realities. The paintings were designed to cater to those art collectors who were hungry for an imaginary, idyllic world during an era of increasing mechanisation and political upheaval. It is ironic that the camera – a technological invention that was part of this modern world – was being used by Hornel to create ideal spaces of escapism.

There is still much to be understood about the way Hornel was

Left. Fig. 97. A Japanese woman in a *kimono* pruning blossom, unidentified photographer, before 1921, Yokohama *shashin* print

Above. Fig. 98. A Kirkcudbright girl posing her hands, attributed to E. A. Hornel, between 1909 and 1933, glass plate negative

Right. Fig. 99. *Playing in the Woods*, E. A. Hornel, 1917, oil on canvas

personally involved in taking the photographs. What is clear is the way he *used* the photographs and how they fit into his artistic practice, and how this stemmed from the people he met and photos he gathered during his initial visit to Japan in 1893. The Japanese aesthetic evident in his collection of photographs changed the way Hornel looked and painted, providing him with an efficient process for creating a successful commercial career.

CHAPTER 6

SRI LANKA, AN OUTSIDER'S GAZE

Heshani Sothiraj Eddleston

Opposite. Fig. 100. A double-exposed glass plate from Sri Lanka with one image of a woman holding a pot on her head and another of several seated people, attributed to E. A. Hornel, 1907, glass plate negative

The portrayal of Sri Lankan communities by 'outsiders' has often taken a clichéd approach. The island was viewed by colonials from a 'position of cultural and political hegemony'.[1] Writers, artists and photographers have documented Sri Lankan inhabitants 'with an eye for the exotic', turning them into marketable objects. Their photographs tried to capture each and every native 'type'. Hornel, much like other colonial artists and photographers, appears to have taken this approach. He used the 'natives' as models to further his painting ambitions – as is evident from his work after his trip to Sri Lanka.

In 1907, Hornel and Elizabeth set sail for Sri Lanka to visit their cousin James Hornell. James worked in the country as a marine biologist for the British government. Hornel's intention was to photograph and paint the pearl fisheries, but the reality made this a challenge. In a letter to a friend, he wrote that it was difficult to paint at the fisheries because of the heat and the smell, but that he was making a 'tremendous lot of studies', which could have meant oil sketches or photographs.[2]

Nearly 350 of Hornel's Sri Lankan photographs survive. Some of them do indeed depict the pearl fisheries on the western coast of the country, but others were taken at tea plantations in the country's elevated interior and in the vicinity of Galle in the south. We know that Hornel travelled to Japan with strong preconceptions of what he expected to find, and his trip to Sri Lanka was no different. Instead of the lush, tropical, idyllic scenery and gardens filled with colour-saturated flowers of his imagination, he found tall trees of coconut, jackfruit and mango, and evergreens that absorbed light and colour, creating a much cooler palette than he had anticipated.[3] Contributing to this cool, green palette were the tea plantations of Sri Lanka's central hills.

In the nineteenth century, when Britain introduced a new political economy based on plantations and mercantile activity to its colonies, trade and society in Sri Lanka changed. The valued items of gems, ivory, elephants and spices took second place initially to coffee and then to tea. It was a Scotsman, James Taylor (1835–1892), who introduced tea to Sri Lanka in 1867. To keep up with the demand, workers from southern India were brought in as cheap labour. They were illiterate, landless, low-caste Tamils from impoverished regions for whom the prospect of work in a foreign land was perceived as a relief.[4]

Although slavery was abolished in 1833 by the British, the lives of the Tamils tied to the plantations in Sri Lanka were little different to those of indentured labourers.[5] Many died before they even reached the plantations, insufficiently fed by the *kangany* (recruiter) who had

Fig. 101. Three Tamil women in Sri Lanka picking tea, attributed to E. A. Hornel, 1907, glass plate negative

persuaded them to travel.[6] Tamil labourers frequently arrived at the plantations heavily in debt to their *kangany*, and a mixture of low wages and part payment in rice rather than money could keep workers tied to their plantation for many years.[7] Due to poor sanitary conditions and an unwillingness to allow labourers to seek medical aid (even after laws were passed to regulate medical care on plantations), the mortality rate among immigrant labourers was high.[8] Not until the 1920s did the Sri Lankan government enact far-reaching changes to the plantation labour system that would benefit its Tamil workers.[9] By this point, approximately one million Tamil plantation labourers had arrived in Sri Lanka. Very little has changed for the workers even now – some plantation workers still live in 'line houses' built more than a hundred years ago.[10]

Above. Fig. 102. A Tamil woman in Sri Lanka seen in three-quarter face, attributed to E. A. Hornel, 1907, glass plate negative

Opposite top. Fig. 103. *Ceylonese Tea Pickers*, E. A. Hornel, 1907–09, oil on canvas

Opposite bottom. Fig. 104. A Tamil woman in Sri Lanka picking tea, attributed to E. A. Hornel, 1907, glass plate negative

It is in this context that Hornel's photographs of the plantation women should be considered. Given the political context, the woman captured in Fig. 102 would not have been able to object to Hornel's wish to photograph her, even if he had asked her permission. There is an inherent power imbalance in these images, one that was typical of how colonial visitors documented Sri Lanka – something that was also visible in their art and writing. The political, cultural and economic power of the colonisers meant that their work was influenced by their privileged position. A common thread in the work of visitors from the late nineteenth to early twentieth centuries, such as Arthur Conan Doyle (1859–1930), Julia Margaret Cameron, Leonard Woolf (1880–1969) and George Bernard Shaw (1856–1950), was to view the Sri Lankans as 'exotic natives', less evolved than Westerners. In a letter to the Indian prime minister Jawaharlal Nehru (1889–1964) written in 1948, Shaw wrote that 'Ceylon is the cradle of the human race because everybody there looks an original'.[11] In keeping with this, Hornel does not photograph the cities of Sri Lanka, but instead focuses on 'natives' in a prelapsarian, rural idyll.

As was common in Western imagery of foreign people at the time, Hornel created 'type' photographs of the women he found on the plantations. 'Racial type' photography became particularly prominent from the 1860s, when the Société d'Ethnographie in Paris and the St Petersburg Academy of Sciences both undertook systematic projects to record 'types'.[12] This genre of photography catered to the Victorian desire to categorise the world, including classifying and illustrating 'the other' through such generalised images.[13]

Fig. 102 can be seen in this context. The Sri Lankan tea picker's face is shown in three-quarter profile, and Hornel captures her traditional jewellery and stretched ear lobe, both markers of her exoticism and traditionally Sri Lankan character. In Hornel's context the repeated head shots of Sri Lankan women were a practical solution for gathering resources for his painted compositions. As an artist who had travelled to Sri Lanka with the intention of finding subjects for his art, such photographs would doubtless have served as studies, similar to a sketch of a life model from various angles.

This approach can be clearly seen in *Ceylonese Tea Pickers* (1907–09, Fig. 103). Consistent with an approach inspired by his 1893–94 trip to Japan, in this painting Hornel has selected models from a variety of his photographs (most notably Figs 101 and 104) and stitched them together in an imagined scene. The faces are obscured, lowered in concentration or covered by shawls. This increases the sense that the identities of the women are being blurred and erased in favour of an 'exotic' ideal. For Hornel, the Tamil tea pickers were merely objects

to be used in his painting to create a commercially viable product.

While the individual identities of Hornel's models are blurred and erased in his paintings, his Sri Lankan photographs reveal a more inherently biased approach. His models come from two distinct communities: the previously mentioned Tamils and the Sinhalese. Hornel's photographs of the two cultures illustrate not only the inherent differences between them (whether he was aware of them or not), but also Hornel's different approaches to the two communities when photographing them.

Hornel has photographed the Sinhalese girl in Fig. 105 quite differently to the Indian Tamil girls in Figs 106 and 107. In her white clothes, the former exudes innocence and virtue, and sits on a dignified mat rather than the bare earth. She also seems to be actively posing for him as opposed to being static or captured at work like the Tamil girls. The Sinhalese community is the dominant group in Sri Lanka, which explains their more active participation in Hornel's photography and

Above left. Fig. 105. A Sinhalese girl in Sri Lanka sitting on a mat, attributed to E. A. Hornel, 1907, glass plate negative

Above right. Fig. 106. A Tamil girl in Sri Lanka sitting on the ground, attributed to E. A. Hornel, 1907, glass plate negative

their more dignified portrayal by him. Hornel's photographic depiction of the two communities responded to and perpetuated existing biases regarding the two communities.

In this, Hornel is typical of how contemporary Westerners perceived the 'native other'. His photographs were created to capture poses to make his paintings different, interesting and saleable in the West. His paintings suggest that Hornel did not consider the cultural or historical nuances of the people he saw, although his photographs reveal an inherent underlying bias. However, to say that Hornel's Sri Lankan photographs reveal a bias in his attitudes is not to criticise unfairly a historical figure from a moralistic modern standpoint. Images and attitudes like Hornel's persist to this day.

Barely twenty years ago, William Dalrymple (b.1965) continued to perpetuate such stereotypes in his book *The Age of Kali*. In it he wrote:

> The Tamils and the Singhalese [*sic*] have been neighbours in Sri Lanka for nearly three thousand years, and throughout much of that time they have been fighting each other. The north and

Fig. 107. A Tamil woman in Sri Lanka surrounded by tea leaves, attributed to E. A. Hornel, 1907, glass plate negative

> east of the island is the preserve of the dark-skinned Tamils: small and sharp and hard-working and Hindu. Elsewhere the island is dominated by the Singhalese [*sic*], a languid and strikingly beautiful race of fair-skinned Buddhists.[14]

Such sweeping generalisations add fuel to existing stereotypes and biases. The idea that one group is more beautiful, more hardworking or more tolerant than the other only cements biases. In Sri Lanka, dark skin is considered unattractive and often a sign of the person being from a lower caste. Light (or 'fair') skin is considered beautiful. This remains apparent in modern Sri Lanka where young men and women try to achieve a lighter skin tone by using facial bleach and other skin-lightening products. Hornel's paintings may have been egalitarian in their anonymisation of his Sri Lankan models, but as is often the way, his photographs expose his unconsious bias.

The importance of colour is perhaps visible in the clothing worn by the two communities. Clothing in Sri Lanka played an important role in defining status, social class and caste. It put people in their place,

Above. Fig. 108. Three Sinhalese girls in Sri Lanka praying before a shrine and two monks, attributed to E. A. Hornel, 1907, glass plate negative

Opposite. Fig. 109. *Lace Makers, Ceylon*, E. A. Hornel, 1908, oil on canvas

defined individuals and determined how others saw them. Sinhalese women, for instance, were supposed to 'avoid any form of clothing, especially short dresses, which could arouse bad passion in men'.[15] Consequently, the Sinhalese girls in Hornel's photographs are almost exclusively dressed in a pure white *lama sariya* (a child's sari – essentially a sarong and jacket as seen in Fig. 105), while the Tamils wear darker, heavily patterned *saris*. Despite this, Hornel seems to have been willing to generally (although not exclusively) treat all the Sri Lankan communities as 'Ceylonese', as illustrated by *Lace Makers, Ceylon* (1908, Fig. 109). The girls in the painting wear the clean, white jackets worn by the Sinhalese in his photographs, but their sarongs are dark and heavily patterned, like those of the Tamils.

In Hornel's photos, some of the Tamil women wear a *sari* blouse underneath their *sari* (such as the woman in Fig. 104), while others are bare-armed and bare-breasted (as in Fig. 107).[16] It is worth noting that explicit nudity features very rarely in Hornel's art (either before or after his visit to Sri Lanka in 1907), so the appearance of the Tamil woman's breast in Fig. 107 was probably not artistically driven. He may simply have been seeking to capture her crouching pose (and

E A Hornel
1908

the exposure was incidental), and the erotic undertones were unintentional. It may have been that a photograph like this was, for Hornel, just a prime example of a 'native' Sri Lankan, as nakedness among colonial subjects has long been associated with 'primitiveness and savagery'.[17] Either way, once again his photographs paint a much more complex picture than his innocent, idyllic paintings.

It is not just through clothing that Hornel's photographs illustrate inherent biases in his attitude towards the Tamils and Sinhalese. The Tamil community pictured in Hornel's photographs appears to be one-dimensional – impoverished, uncultured labourers. In contrast, the Sinhalese appear to be multi-dimensional, being photographed participating in a variety of cultural activities such as praying, playing music and lace-making. It is unclear whether Hornel intentionally photographed Tamils and Sinhalese according to preconceived stereotypes, or whether his access to people and places was limited, forcing him to portray the communities in a restricted way. For example, there are no images of middle-class or wealthy Tamils.

Hornel also photographed Sinhalese girls undertaking more refined work than the Tamils, yet his photographs and subsequent paintings

Fig. 110. Three Sinhalese women in Sri Lanka undertaking *beeralu* lace-making in front of a house, attributed to E. A. Hornel, 1907, glass plate negative

Fig. 111. A Sinhalese girl in Sri Lanka undertaking *beeralu* lace-making, attributed to E. A. Hornel, 1907, glass plate negative

Fig. 112. Five Sinhalese girls in Sri Lanka playing the *rabana*, attributed to E. A. Hornel, 1907, glass plate negative

still erase cultural nuances. Figs 110 and 111 are of *beeralu* lace-making, a form of lace-making particularly associated with Galle in Sri Lanka. However, Fig. 111 shows a child undertaking the activity. Judging by other photographs contemporaneous with Hornel's visit, children did not usually carry out *beeralu* lace-making. Photographic documentation of lace-makers usually shows older women such as those in Fig. 110. This, and the fact the models are so smartly dressed, makes it possible that these scenes were staged for Hornel.

Hornel required these performative photographs to compose his commercially successful paintings. Youthful girls in natural surroundings were his subject matter and the lace-making was simply a way of

Above. Fig. 113. A girl in Sri Lanka carrying a water jar, attributed to E. A. Hornel, 1907, glass plate negative

Right. Fig. 114. *Ceylon Water Pots*, E. A. Hornel, 1907–09, oil on canvas

organising their bodies around a social task. His painting *Lace Makers, Ceylon* uses poses from several photographs to create an ideal version of an exotic activity. What audiences would not have known is that the painting may depict more than lace-making, as Hornel also appears to have used poses from Fig. 112, which captures a group playing the *rabana* – a one-sided hand drum played on special occasions or during the Sinhala New Year festivities. Similar to *beeralu* lace-making, playing the *rabana* is a way for women to get together, sing, recite *kavi* (poetry) and bond. *Lace Makers, Ceylon* may look like a plausible scene, but in fact ignores several nuances visible in the photographs. The painting

Above left. Fig. 115. A Kirkcudbright girl resting her hand on a water jar, attributed to E. A. Hornel, between 1907 and 1910, glass plate negative

Above right. Fig. 116. A Sinhalese girl in Sri Lanka, possibly flying a kite, attributed to E. A. Hornel, 1907, glass plate negative

even blends two completely different activities, emphasising how Hornel used Sri Lankan women and girls, whether Tamil or Sinhalese, as mere props for his art, just as he did in Japan, Myanmar and Scotland.

Indeed, Hornel did not just use these women and girls as props in his subsequent paintings of Sri Lanka. He ensured that he had a constant supply of 'exotic' Sri Lankan poses by encouraging his Scottish models to mimic their Sri Lankan peers. In this way, the influence of his visit to Sri Lanka, and the photographs he took there, can be seen throughout all of his subsequent art.

CHAPTER 7

HORNEL IN MYANMAR

Ben Reiss and Antonia Laurence-Allen

Opposite. Detail from Fig. 129. A Myanmar dancer in white on a floral rug with her left arm raised, facing the camera, attributed to E. A. Hornel, 1920, glass plate negative

Hornel's collection of images from Myanmar comprises the smallest part of his photographic collection. A bare two dozen are present, almost exclusively portraying traditional dancers from the city of Mandalay. They were taken at the end of 1920, when Hornel and Elizabeth spent three months in the country as part of a year-long trip around the world that would also take them to Japan, Canada and America.[1] Hornel may have been at least in part inspired to visit after reading some of the many travelogues published on Myanmar around 1900, which catered to travellers wishing to discover 'exotic' mystery.

One such example is *Picturesque Burma* (1897) by Alice Hart (née Rowland, 1848–1931).[2] Hart describes the country as 'little known to tourists',[3] suggesting at least part of its appeal was in its mysterious nature. She calls Myanmar 'a land of delight', offering 'to the artist the harmonious "composition" of the scenery of river, forest, and mountain, the picturesqueness of the flower-clad people, and the splendour of the colouring of sky and land'.[4]

Hart goes on to talk at length about the Irrawaddy – a significant

Below left. Fig. 117. Two Myanmar dancers standing on mats in front of a white backdrop, attributed to E. A. Hornel, 1920, glass plate negative

Below right. Fig. 118. A Kirkcudbright girl posing in the form of a Myanmar dancer in front of picture frames in the studio at Broughton House, attributed to E. A. Hornel, between 1921 and 1927, glass plate negative

Opposite. Fig. 119. *Burmese Musicians and Dancers*, E. A. Hornel, c.1922–27, oil on canvas

Opposite. Fig. 120. *Japanese Dancers*, E. A. Hornel, 1921–25, oil on canvas

Above left. Fig. 121. Two Myanmar dancers standing on boards in front of a painted backdrop, attributed to E. A. Hornel, 1920, glass plate negative

Above right. Fig. 122. A Kirkcudbright girl posing in front of an easel and paintings in the studio at Broughton House, attributed to E. A. Hornel, *c.*1906–10, glass plate negative

waterway that runs the length of Myanmar – in language seemingly chosen to appeal directly to artists. She lingers most romantically on imagery of women collecting water:

> From the bamboo houses, built on piles in the village on the hill, stream out in twos and ones the village maidens, clad in clinging rainbow-tinted garments, and with red clay water-jars on their heads. They come down to the river-side, walk unconcernedly into the water, fill their jars, or take their morning dip, still modestly clothed, and each girl is a picture, classic in form, oriental in colour.[5]

Hart also dedicates an entire chapter (illustrated with drawings and photographs) to music, dancing and acting. She notes the restrictive clothing of the dancers, and particularly describes their flexibility and the contortions of their arms.[6]

Hart's descriptions illustrate tropes that were consistently repeated in travel writing about Myanmar. In *A Bachelor Girl in Burma* (1907), G. E. Mitton (1868–1955) is less complimentary about the dancing than Hart ('not in the least what Europeans call dancing') but included

Above left. Fig. 123. A Myanmar dancer in white kneeling on a floral rug, facing the camera, attributed to E. A. Hornel, 1920, glass plate negative

Above right. Fig. 124. A Myanmar dancer in white on a floral rug, facing away from the camera, attributed to E. A. Hornel, 1920, glass plate negative

numerous photos of the Irrawaddy.[7] Photographs of dancers and dancing occur several times in *The Silken East* (1904) by V. C. Scott O'Connor (1869–1945), in which the Irrawaddy is also a constant presence.[8]

Local dancers were also a prominent subject of painter Sir Gerald Kelly (1879–1972), who visited Myanmar from 1908 to 1909, executing a large number of paintings and sketches of the 'charming young ladies' of Mandalay.[9] Unlike many contemporary chroniclers, however, Kelly named his models. A portrayal of Ma Si Gyaw (1909–14) is in the Tate's collection, for example, and Kelly frequently sketched another dancer, Ma Seyn Mé.[10] Kelly's depictions of these women were described by his friend William Somerset Maugham as having 'a strange impenetrability, their gestures are enigmatic and yet significant, they are charming'.[11]

As with his initial visit to Japan, Hornel seems to have travelled to Myanmar with a preconception of what he was looking for, this time possibly inspired by his Japanese experiences. Indeed, he seems to have pre-empted some of the forms that he would find in Myanmar with

Fig. 125. *Memories of Mandalay*, E. A. Hornel, 1923, oil on canvas

earlier photographs of girls in Kirkcudbright (compare Figs 121 and 122). While in Myanmar, he wrote that he hoped to gather material to create 'a picture which would be very Burmese, dancing girls & Peacocks', an idea he had had in mind for 'many years'.[12] Two local artists took him to a theatre and introduced him to the manager, who paraded his best dancers for Hornel so that he could study and photograph them.[13] It is possible that Hornel met these artists through the Burma Art Club, an artistic network which, like the Photographic Society of Japan and Meiji Fine Arts Society, contained both local and British members. He went on to paint his 'dancing girls & Peacocks' in

Left. Fig. 126. *Burmese Maidens*, E. A. Hornel, *c.*1922–27, oil on canvas

Above. Fig. 127. A Kirkcudbright girl crouching in the form of a Myanmar dancer in the studio at Broughton House, attributed to E. A. Hornel, between 1921 and 1927, glass plate negative

Fig. 128. *Girls Picking Blue Flax*, E. A. Hornel, 1917, oil on canvas

Memories of Mandalay (1923, Fig. 125) and produced a number of other representations of Myanmar dancers, sometimes using the vertical format and flattened composition he had learnt from Yokohama *shashin*.

Hornel's paintings conformed to the emerging Western impressions of dancing girls in Myanmar (as illustrated in text and image by Hart and Kelly above), most especially with his focus on arm and upper body movements. Like Kelly, Hornel seems intrigued with the 'enigmatic' gestures of the Myanmar dancers. It is worth contrasting Hornel's anonymising, frantic approach with Kelly's more composed named portraits of individual dancers. We know Hornel was interested in the movements of the Japanese dancers he photographed in 1893–94, and that he encouraged his Kirkcudbright models to copy their poses. Equally, the sharply cocked hands and arms of the Myanmar dancers – executing a particular style of dancing that imitates the jerky

Above left. Fig. 129. A Myanmar dancer in white on a floral rug with her left arm raised, facing the camera, attributed to E. A. Hornel, 1920, glass plate negative

Above right. Fig. 130. A Kirkcudbright girl posing in the form of a Myanmar dancer on a cushion in the studio at Broughton House, attributed to E. A. Hornel, between 1921 and 1927, glass plate negative

movements of a puppet, with legs and arms strongly bent as if being manipulated by strings – must also have appealed to his artistic eye. Their movements seem to have been incorporated into his later paintings of Scottish subjects.

Hornel had always had an interest in the hands and feet of his models. In paintings like *Seashore Roses* (*c.*1907, Fig. 93) and *Girls Picking Blue Flax* (1917, Fig. 128), the hands of his Scottish models are the focus of each painting, reaching towards the centre and drawing the eye. However, they look relaxed and relatively naturalistic.

Looking ahead at his later paintings from the 1920s, we see a subtly different treatment of hands and arms. This is clearly illustrated by *Balloons and Blossom, Brighouse Bay* (*c.*1927–33, Fig. 131). Every visible arm of the three models is bent at either the wrist or the elbow or both. Rather than reaching for the centre of the composition, the arms now bend up and away. It seems likely Hornel achieved this effect by encouraging his Scottish models to mimic the poses of Myanmar dancers, as evidenced by the photographic collection. The girl on the

Fig. 131. *Balloons and Blossom, Brighouse Bay*, E. A. Hornel, *c.*1927–33, oil on canvas

left of *Balloons and Blossom, Brighouse Bay* appears to have been painted from the Kirkcudbright model in Fig. 130, who in turn seems to be mimicking the Myanmar dancer in Fig. 129. The exaggerated, sharply angled wrists of the two girls on the right of *Balloons and Blossom, Brighouse Bay* are rarely seen in Hornel's paintings completed before his visit to Myanmar. In this way, we can see that, although small, his

Left. Fig. 132. *Water Carriers on the Banks of the Irrawaddy*, E. A. Hornel, 1923, oil on canvas

Above. Fig. 133. A Sinhalese woman bathing, attributed to E. A. Hornel, 1907, glass plate negative

Fig. 134. A Japanese woman wearing a *kimono* and holding a parasol, unidentified photographer, before 1921, photographic print

collection of photos of Myanmar dancers added a significant new gesture to the range of poses he used to create his Scottish paintings.

Although there are no photographs of the Irrawaddy in the Hornel collection, several of his paintings feature water carriers on its banks, as so evocatively described by Hart in 1897. What is particularly interesting about these paintings is their lack of photographic model. By the 1920s, Hornel rarely deviated from his commercially successful method of creating compositions by stitching together poses taken from photographs. Without photos of women on the banks of the Irrawaddy, he had to look elsewhere for his models.

For figures in paintings such as *Water Carriers on the Banks of the Irrawaddy* (1923, Fig. 132), he instead turned to his collection of Sri Lankan photos, which contains a number of images of women bathing in, collecting and carrying water (Fig. 133). He may even have drawn

Above left. Fig. 135. Two Sri Lankan women sorting through tea, attributed to E. A. Hornel, 1907, glass plate negative

Above right. Fig. 136. Myanmar dancer and musician standing in front of a white backdrop, attributed to E. A. Hornel, 1920, glass plate negative

Opposite. Fig. 137. *Burmese Water Carriers on the Banks of the Irrawaddy*, E. A. Hornel, *c.*1922–27, oil on canvas

on some of his Japanese photographs as well (Fig. 134). *Burmese Water Carriers on the Banks of the Irrawaddy* (*c.*1922–27, Fig. 137) shows a similar willingness to mix activity as well as nationality in his creation of an exotic ideal, as a tea picker from Sri Lanka and a musician from Myanmar combine to depict Irrawaddy water carriers (Figs 135 and 136).[14]

This conflation of multiple cultures by Hornel demonstrates two things. First, it illustrates how Hornel used photographs to compose his paintings, selecting a pose from any photograph because it fitted the composition, rather than aiming for fidelity. Second, it follows that Hornel was not interested in the individuality of the women in his photographs or their cultural settings. He was simply working with stereotypes like 'exotic native in foreign land' or 'rural peasant at one with nature'. In Hornel's Myanmar paintings, 'the Irrawaddy' becomes little more than an exotic hook in the title. The commercial appeal of these paintings would no doubt have been enhanced by the fact 'Burma' was relatively unknown to outsiders. In the contorted limbs of Myanmar's dancing girls, and the 'picture, classic in form, oriental in colour' presented by women on the banks of the Irrawaddy, Hornel found new poses that would enhance his popular paintings of women and girls.

CHAPTER 8

JAPAN: A SOURCE OF INSPIRATION FOR HISTORIC GARDENS IN SCOTLAND

Jill Raggett

Opposite. Fig. 138. A Japanese woman standing beneath blossom, Tamamura Kōzaburō, between 1883 and 1921, Yokohama *shashin* print

Hornel was not alone in wanting to add a 'touch of Japan' to his garden at Broughton House. Others in the British Isles were inspired to do the same, motivated by travels to Japan or by enthusiastically embracing the fashion for Japonisme. However, those gardens created in Scotland had the advantage of climate and landscape; the damp climate, wind-sculpted trees and rocky coastlines all mirror the conditions and landscapes that inspired many of the iconic gardens of Japan. The Japanese-style gardens of the late Victorian and early Edwardian eras were rarely accurate representations of the diverse gardens of Japan, but through the addition of plants, ornaments and other features conjured up an image of Japan in the mind of the viewer.

A variety of motivations resulted in the creation of Japanese-style gardens in Britain, including the opening of Japan to the West, the subsequent influences of the Japanese arts, new plant introductions and international exhibitions. However, the major inspiration for these gardens came from travellers visiting Japan and their resulting desire for a Japanese garden as a fashionable addition to an estate or even as a commercial enterprise such as a tea garden. Japanese-style gardens were created as holiday mementoes on the estates of those who could afford to travel to Japan, often returning with the appropriate ornaments and even plants.

By the time Hornel purchased his eighteenth-century town house in 1900, on the High Street in Kirkcudbright, other Japanese-style gardens had been created in Scotland. After Colonel Charles Anstruther-Thomson (1855–1925) returned from visiting Japan in 1892, he had a Japanese garden created at his property Charleton House, Fife. The garden was centred on a pond, with painted features including a Shinto shrine[1] – Shinto is the animistic belief system in Japan. Japanese travels inspired George Bullough (1870–1939) to do likewise at his summer residence, Kinloch Castle on the island of Rum, *c.*1905, with a garden laid out either side of a rocky stream, a Japanese-inspired bridge, stone lanterns and what has been described as an 'elaborate planting'.[2]

The addition of Japanese garden features and plants was a way of signifying to the garden visitor that they were to be transported to Japan. At Manderston House, Berwickshire, *c.*1900, Japanese stone lanterns and a stone pagoda were placed at the end of a lake in what was considered a suitable setting.[3] In some cases, these features and plants would result in an area of the garden being renamed. Around 1895 at Arbigland, Dumfries (not far from Kirkcudbright), there was the creation of a glade of *Acer palmatum* (Japanese maple) and *Prunus* (cherry) trees in the woodland garden by the lake, in an area which

Opposite. Fig. 139. 'The young fellow is enjoying the sweets beside the cherry blossoms at Kobe', Tamamura Kōzaburō, between 1883 and 1921, Yokohama *shashin* print

became known as 'Japan'.[4] The same was true of the gardens created by Osgood Mackenzie (1842–1922) at Inverewe in the Highlands (now cared for by the National Trust for Scotland), where, by around 1900, part of the garden was known as 'Japan'. It contained a Japanese cherry tree and a planting of bamboo, the latter aptly named the Bamboose-lem.[5] Bamboo is a plant rarely used in the gardens of Japan due to its invasive nature, but is often seen growing in the surrounding land-scape.

There were more complex Japanese-style gardens being created in the early 1900s, resulting from a greater enthusiasm or deeper knowl-edge of the culture and artistic traditions of Japan by the gardens' creators. At Dundarach, Perthshire, *c.*1906, John Henry Dixon (1838–1926) developed a Japanese garden that included a range of features with a *torii* gateway leading to a shrine building, stone lanterns, and a pond complete with waterlilies – Dixon knew that the characteristic lotus would not flourish in the Scottish climate.[6] Dixon had lived in Japan and he planted species that might be found there. The garden even included a miniature Mount Fuji, complete with snow-covered peak made from the local Pitlochry white spar rock.

In the same decade as the creation of the garden at Dundarach, Ella Christie (1861–1949) returned from Japan and employed a Japanese woman, Handa Taki (1871–1956), a student of horticulture in England, to help her create the garden of Sha Raku En (the place of pleasure and delight) at Cowden Castle in Clackmannanshire. Christie was able to consult the writings and illustrations of Josiah Conder, as she owned a copy of his book *Landscape Gardening in Japan* (1893).[7] Conder was British but lived and worked in Japan, having been recruited by the Meiji government as a *yatoi* (hired foreigner) for the role of Professor of Architecture for the Imperial College of Engineering in Tokyo. Less than ten years after his arrival in Japan, Conder gave a lecture to the Asiatic Society of Japan on 5 May 1886, entitled 'The Art of Landscape Gardening in Japan'.[8] The notes for this talk seem to have formed the basis for his later publication. The ideal garden in Japan was described by Conder in his 1893 book as 'a retreat for secluded ease and medi-tation' and not a display of the owner's wealth, the latter resulting in an overcrowded appearance with too many rare rocks and plants. He saw the dangers of many of the Japanese-style gardens becoming over-ornamented trophies of wealthy travellers, showing a lack of sensitivity in the reinterpretation of the gardens of Japan.

Conder can be considered an important bridge between the two cultures with his professional interests in architecture and gardens. His book was the first major publication in English on the topic of the gardens of Japan and could be used for guidance regarding authenticity.

Opposite. Fig. 140. Apple Blossom, E. A. Hornel, probably between 1921 and 1933, oil on canvas

Above. Fig. 141. A Japanese woman in a *kimono* standing next to a tree, unidentified photographer, before 1921, Yokohama *shashin* print

Fig. 142. *Jinrikisha* on a street beneath blossom, attributed to Tamamura Kōzaburō, between 1883 and 1921, Yokohama *shashin* print

However, his large green book in two volumes was more frequently used as a 'pick and mix', where readers selected features from the illustrations to be recreated on their estates, often using the skills of their own staff, rather than developing a deeper understanding of the design principles and the culture that had bought about the gardens of Japan. Conder was aware of this; he realised that gardens made in other countries would not be replica copies of those in Japan, and that they would be gardens created far from the geology, climate, society and culture that had led to their distinctive appearance. He saw it as inevitable for gardens 'transferred to a foreign clime where landscape presents itself in a different garb, and regarded by people who interpret nature in another manner' that 'these lovely gardens can hardly fail to appear as examples of quaint and fanciful conceit'.[9]

As well as Conder, garden owners and makers could turn to the writing and watercolours of Ella Du Cane (1874–1943, published in *The Flowers and Gardens of Japan*, 1908[10]) and Walter Tyndale (1855–1943, published in Harriet Taylour's *Japanese Gardens*, 1912[11]), and the romantic photographs of Japanese gardens by Herbert Ponting (1870–1935, published in the *Illustrated London News*, 1907[12]). The Japanese-style gardens were the result of cultural borrowing, producing a picture of what the owner felt was 'Japanese' – a composite image of Japan. Sometimes they were a visual scrapbook of their visit to the country.

Those created in Scotland were frequently the archetypal, early Japanese-style garden, based around an irregular water feature that

Fig. 143. A plan and features for a Japanese garden, unknown artist, from T. W. Sanders, *The Flower Garden* (London: W. H. & L. Collingridge, 1907, p. 34), image author's own

was outlined with rocks and included areas for irises and waterlilies. The water would be crossed by at least one bridge, possibly a representation of the red arching bridge at Nikko, a stone slab or stepping stones. The bridges were part of a network of informal paths, ideally created of large flat stones that surrounded pools and various features. The gardens may also have included a tea house which, like the bridges, was either imported from Japan or of local origin. In more elaborate gardens, they might also have included a temple, shrine or traditional Japanese red *torii* entrance gateway. Japanese stone lanterns recalled those maybe seen at Nara. Bronze statuary of cranes, dragon-encircled bowls and *bonsai* provided additional ornamentation. These gardens could become quite crowded and often seemed to lack the simplicity and distillation of nature that had inspired their original counterparts in Japan.

The phenomena of 'Japanese gardens' were so much part of British gardening in the early twentieth century that the successful gardening author Thomas William Sanders (1855–1926) included them in a section of *The Flower Garden*, published in 1907. Sanders felt that such gardens were only possible 'in large gardens where there is plenty of scope to form the miniature lakes and make the miniature undulations of surface'. The lakes required an irregular outline, surrounded by a path and crossed with a rustic bridge, with Japanese plants placed in groups, and a 'summer house or two … in convenient spots to view the garden'.[13] The Japanese garden suggested by Sanders combined

Fig. 144. Stepping stones and Japanese-style bridge in the garden at Broughton House, Brian and Nina Chapple, 2008, digital photograph, © Brian & Nina Chapple

collections of Japanese plants, including bamboo avenues, plenty of almonds, cherries and lilies, with features that had become popular such as miniature pines on an 'elevated knoll'. The planning of such a garden made no consideration for the context of the site except for its size and the need for a screening of plants so that it could not be observed from the rest of the garden.[14] A plan and the features, including an arched bridge, *bonsai* and stepping stones, were illustrated within the text (Fig. 143).

The question of the authenticity of Japanese-style gardens ran through the contemporary literature but, despite reservations, in 1909 'the reign of the Japanese garden' was seen by a writer in the *Gardeners' Magazine* to be 'a very real and lasting one' with a 'decided trend toward the Japanese style of garden ornament'.[15] Certainly it was a valid observation, as Japanese-style gardens, with their informal design, had successfully managed to integrate with other garden styles popular at

Fig. 145. Blossom in the garden at Broughton House, Brian and Nina Chapple, 2010, digital photograph, © Brian & Nina Chapple

the time such as naturalistic woodland or water gardens – this was the case in several of the Scottish gardens. At the end of the decade, the gardens of Japan were promoted at the 1910 Japan–British Exhibition, in London. At this popular show, the Japanese government built two large-scale gardens, which they sought to make as authentic as possible, and these continued the fashion for Japanese-style gardens into the twentieth century. The Kyoto Exhibitors' Association at the 1910 Japan–British Exhibition was aware of the demand from foreign visitors for items such as 'stone or bronze lanterns, bridges, and rocks', which were taken home 'to decorate gardens on strange soil'.[16]

So, where does Hornel's garden at Broughton House fit in the emerging story of these idiosyncratic Japanese-style Scottish gardens, which were themselves a product of the late nineteenth-century interest in everything Japanese? First, Hornel remodelled the house, but by 1916 there was a description which showed that Hornel had created

Fig. 146. Photograph of the informal pool crossed by stepping stones in the garden of Broughton House. Dorothy McBirnie, from *The Studio Year-book of Decorative Art* (London: The Studio, 1925, p. 181)

a garden differing from what was typically expected for a domestic garden. It was considered to display a 'wild civility' and there was 'an unobtrusive miniature lake, with clusters of polyanthus, mounds of stone, trees laden with white and pink blossom'.[17] The potential Japanese influence could be seen in the informal stone-edged pool crossed with irregular stepping stones, which appeared in *The Studio Year-book of Decorative Art* of 1925.[18] At some point, a statue of a crane appeared in the pool[19] – this might have been purchased by Hornel when he went to Japan for a second time, in 1921, as a memento of that visit. However, the sculpture was probably a later addition as it was not featured in the 1925 photographic record.

The planting of the garden included species from Japan, a wisteria that may have been planted by Hornel and a collection of tree peonies added in the 1920s.[20] Again, these could be a result of Hornel's second visit to Japan. He and his sister had an interest in a range of Japanese plants including bamboos, cherries, lilies, Japanese irises and peonies. This can be seen from surviving nursery catalogues in the Hornel Archive. These catalogues were from the Yokohama Nursery Company that welcomed many overseas visitors to their premises in Japan. The company supplied these visitors with a wide range of plants, including *bonsai* and garden ornaments, all attractively and temptingly illustrated in their English-language catalogues.

It is interesting to consider that this author has found no evidence that Hornel ever called his garden at Broughton House 'Japanese'. While his sensitivities for the gardens and arts of Japan may have led to a more informal planting, as well as directing his plant selection, he did not include signifiers such as stone lanterns. This could be considered a garden influenced by Japan rather than one that was created to resemble those found in Japan. The garden's connection to Japan was augmented after Hornel's death as a celebration or remembrance of his connection with that country and the success it played in his artistic career. In the 1990s, a red bridge (Fig. 144) was added by a gardener over the small rock-edged pool to aid public safety in crossing what had become known as the Japanese pond.

Historical authenticity is a challenge for gardens, as they are not fixed objects but a series of processes. The constant dynamic of plant growth, weathering and maintenance decisions will lead to changes. In addition, Japanese-style gardens are frequently considered 'not very Japanese', and owners or garden keepers with the best of intentions often try to restore these records of the past to a more twenty-first-century viewpoint of the gardens of Japan. At times, the allure of Japan seems to hold a magnetic force and gardens are restored, given additions or reimagined in ways not envisaged by a past maker. The

Fig. 147. Japanese elements (including a crane) in the garden at Broughton House, Brian and Nina Chapple, 2012, digital photograph, © Brian & Nina Chapple

historical Japanese-style garden is best viewed with the surviving archival and physical evidence, through the eyes of its contemporary creators, builders and garden visitors, both for its management and a sensitive understanding of the complex histories it represents. The building of gardens inspired by Japan in Scotland is an ongoing tradition, with more being designed and built in the twentieth and twenty-first centuries; examples include Attadale in Wester Ross, and at the St Mungo Museum of Religious Life and Art in Glasgow.[21] The fascination, inspiration and influence of Japan that was part of Hornel's life continues to be part of the creative process of garden making.

CHAPTER 9

HORNEL AT HOME: BROUGHTON HOUSE & GARDEN, 1900–33

Samuel Gallacher

Opposite. Fig. 148. John Keppie, Hornel, Philip Halstead and Elizabeth, T. & R. Annan & Sons, c.1930, photographic print

Fig. 149. Picture Gallery, Broughton House, T. & R. Annan & Sons, 1916, photographic print

In a photograph dating from around 1930 (Fig. 148), we see Hornel at home in Kirkcudbright, Galloway, standing beside a magnificent fireplace, his hand resting against the stonework – the very embodiment of a gentleman of his era. His sister Elizabeth gazes at him from the far right; between them sits the pianist Philip Halstead, a leading member of the Glasgow Art Club, while another friend, the architect John Keppie, sits to the far left. This posed assemblage, set against the backdrop of the fireplace, a glazed bookcase and just a hint of mahogany panelling, would seem at first little more than a typical photograph of an upper-class social group in a grand drawing room of a country mansion. On closer inspection, we start to see more curious elements: on the mantelpiece, an antique bust is flanked by a statuette of the Buddha. Had the photographer decided on a wider shot, the space would have been revealed in its entirety. We would see Hornel's artworks on the walls, rich in colour and inspired by the landscape of his native Galloway, as well as his travels to Sri Lanka, Japan and Myanmar; between the paintings are busts by Auguste Rodin and others; and above them all, a plasterwork frieze of the Parthenon marbles encircling the room. This eclecticism is by Hornel's design and reflects the complexity of the man himself, for this room is no ordinary drawing room but a gallery extension purpose-built by Hornel and designed by Keppie. This space surprises visitors today as it would no doubt have impressed Hornel's guests. It underlines the importance of appreciating Hornel's house and garden in Kirkcudbright as a source from which to add to our understanding of Hornel himself.

When Hornel purchased Broughton House, he was acquiring arguably the grandest house in the town, one with a distinct and noble history. Built as a townhouse for an important local family, the Murrays of Broughton and Cally, in around 1734 (though Hornel believed it to be older still), the house was then unique, being set back and raised from Kirkcudbright High Street, terraced by numbers 10 and 14 to either side. A succession of owners, including the Earls of Selkirk, all left their marks. Most notably, in the early nineteenth century, the Melville family raised the roof for new servants' quarters, installed Regency interiors in the main public rooms, and integrated Broughton House with neighbouring 10 High Street, creating the beginning of the much larger property we know today. Throughout this period, the long garden, which stretches to the River Dee, was remodelled. Ordnance Survey maps detail its formal layout, in the fashion of the times. Having returned from his expedition in Japan in February 1894, Hornel had been living with his sister Margaret (1855–1938) and brother-in-law William Mouncey (1852–1901) at 19 High Street, leasing a studio next door at number 21.[1] Hornel's friend, the artist E. A. Taylor, recalled visiting this studio:

> My first visit to Kirkcudbright was my first lone holiday, as well as my first visit to an artist's studio, that of E. A. Hornel: to recall it is to feel again the thrill of artistic desire, the impetus to explore, the adventure of the conquest of happiness. Around him was a wealth of colour and above the doorway, a dead peacock, which was inspiring the arrangement of blue and green of the canvas on which he was at work.[2]

For Hornel, his studio space was clearly an important element of his creative process. It was a place of invention and inspiration, a place to host (and impress) visitors and to display his already exotic and curious collections. The possibility of purchasing Broughton House arose in 1900, offering Hornel the opportunity to combine domestic, artistic and social spaces to better suit his lifestyle. He completed the purchase of Broughton House on 3 September 1900;[3] just over three months later, on 8 December, Keppie completed his first designs for a radical new purpose-built gallery and studio extension.[4]

In 1916, the journalist James Shaw Simpson visited Broughton House, profiling the property for *Scottish Country Life*.[5] Hornel himself conducted the tour with the air of a museum guide, imparting stories about objects in the house and their rumoured provenances. The centrepiece was the gallery, 'with monumental fireplace and Parthenon facsimile', which so effectively showcased both Hornel's work and choice pieces from his wider collection. Simpson later reflected: 'His house at Kirkcudbright, as I wrote some years ago, is a treasury of art, impeccable taste, and irresistible effects. It is the external efflorescence of the soul of the painter whose joyous creations have profoundly enlarged the aesthetic vision of the race.'[6]

The gallery which had so impressed Simpson in 1916 was then only six years old, but already it was clear that Hornel's massive extension to the historic Broughton House and the display of collections were viewed by the visiting writer as a clear representation of Hornel himself. Although Keppie's first designs were already complete by December 1900, it was not until January 1909 that the final design (not much changed) was confirmed.[7] The impact of the gallery was emphasised by the transition from the reception hall – with all its cluttered, genteel domestic charm – leading into the new space, austere, classical and bright (Fig. 149). Keppie's 1909 designs reveal additional details. In the basement a heating chamber housed a boiler, and radiators were discreetly stationed in the panelled gallery above.

This was a domestic space and a commercial gallery. It was a sitting room with an Erard piano in the corner – as there is today – played, one might imagine, by Hornel's talented friend, Halstead.[8] It was also a commercial space to display Hornel's artworks to friends and clients (only his own works hung on the walls); a photograph from *c.*1911 shows Hornel studying his work alongside fellow members of the 'Glasgow School' (Fig. 150). Hornel's picture gallery at Broughton House was always intended to relate directly to the other space created by Keppie's extension, his studio. Exiting the gallery, visitors would walk onto a gantry, overlooking the double-height studio. The roof lights provided ample illumination, well suited for his use of the studio

Fig. 150. Hornel, John Keppie and two others in front of *The Earth's Awakening*, 1909 (sold that year to Dundee City Art Gallery), in the Broughton House Gallery, Malcolm Harper, 1911, photographic print

to photograph his models. Continuing Hornel's use of his old studio at 21 High Street, the new studio was designed as a comfortable domestic and social space. Even from the outset in around 1910, in a photograph (Fig. 151) we see Hornel with his sisters around the stove, his palette hung above as though a hunting trophy, his paintings and unused frames clumsily surrounding them. Indeed, his framed paintings, which we so often see stacked up in the studio at the edges of photographs of his young female models, seemed to have been stored in the studio, out of sight, but ready to be shown. A novel addition since the original 1900 design, the 1909 design features a large trapdoor from the picture gallery into a basement storeroom not far from the studio. This is shown in Keppie's plans on the right-hand side of the room, but in reality was instead more practically situated in the centre, and was used to move paintings back and forth between the studio and the gallery. Hornel was more than just guide, he was also curator and dealer; the gallery includes a novel dado rail, with pre-made holes

Fig. 151. Elizabeth, Hornel, Margaret Mouncey (née Hornel) and one of Hornel's nieces at Broughton House, unidentified photographer, c.1910, photographic print

allowing for paintings of various dimensions to be hung quickly and changed easily.

Hornel's studio also provides a connection to arguably one of his greatest inspirations: his garden, which was accessed by a pair of glazed doors. Hornel clearly viewed the development of the garden and the house as part of a single project, writing to his friend, the publisher and book collector Thomas Fraser in 1907, 'I daresay you would smile if you could hear all the great schemes Miss H [Elizabeth Hornel] and I are evolving for Broughton House and its garden.'[9] The long garden, already comprising the garden strips of both 10 and 12 High Street, was further enlarged by Hornel when he purchased neighbouring 14 High Street in 1910, annexing most of the garden to his own. Most famously, this project revolved around the creation of a Japanese-inspired garden to the left of the new gallery/studio extension, as shown in a photograph in the 1916 *Scottish Country Life* article. In more detail, Hornel's garden was also subject to a photographic study by Dorothy McBirnie, who visited Hornel and Elizabeth in 1926. She presented Hornel with an album of 20 photographs of the garden, including familial snapshots of each of them, alone or together, and accompanied by a poetic description of the visit.[10] Comparing these to the few photographs of Japanese gardens that Hornel brought back with him from his travels, we can see that Hornel took inspiration from the Japanese images (see Jill Raggett, Chapter 8). His own garden became a pastiche of what he saw as key features and elements – such as stepping stones and wisteria – that he saw and collected photos of in Japan (compare Figs 146, 147 and 152).[11] As Marion Mako found in her comprehensive study of the garden for the National Trust for Scotland, Hornel, despite his bibliophilism, owned none of the classical texts on Japanese horticulture.[12] Instead, his references are principally visual. Indeed, Hornel's own collection of photography includes numerous botanical studies, many of which may be from his own garden, and are no doubt reflected in the rich floral backgrounds which came to dominate his later works that he painted at Broughton House. Fittingly, in the series of photographs of his young models, the garden too was used as an extension of the studio (Fig. 153).

It is difficult to pinpoint when Hornel became an antiquarian. His interest in history is neatly documented in a lecture he delivered in 1888 to the Kirkcudbright Field Naturalists and Antiquarian Society on sixteenth-century Kirkcudbright.[13] He was a member of the town's Stewartry Museum from 1895. In some 1920s photographs taken in his studio, large bookcases are evident. These housed the local-interest Maxwellknowe Collection that he had started to acquire from March 1919 with the help of his friend Fraser.[14] By 1920, the intention of these purchases and the future of his house were made clear in the deeds of trust Hornel had his solicitor draw up:

> It is my wish and intention that Broughton House aforesaid with studio and offices and with all its furnishings and my library, curios, works of art, and other articles therein should be preserved for the purpose of a Public Art Gallery and Library for the benefit of the inhabitants of the Stewartry of Kirkcudbright.[15]

Broughton House was to be his legacy. As he wrote to his friend Fraser a year later, 'I think both of us have the same ideal in front of us, the creation of as perfect a local library as it is possible to make and establish for all times.'[16] After Hornel's death in 1933, Elizabeth made almost

Above. Fig. 152. 'Garden Fujiya Hotel', unidentified photographer, before 1921, photographic postcard

Opposite. Fig. 153. A Kirkcudbright girl holding on to the railings in the Broughton House Garden, attributed to E. A. Hornel, 1920s, glass plate negative

no changes to the property. The creation of the Hornel Trust in 1951 succeeded in fulfilling Hornel's bequest by opening a public reading room in the dining room. But it struggled to meet the financial obligations of maintaining a historic house and garden, and entrusted the house, its collections and garden to the National Trust for Scotland in 1997.

The photographs of Hornel at home reveal a man who had developed his house into the physical embodiment of his own life and interests. As modern visitors find, very little has changed at this charming and intriguing house. Simpson's statement that Broughton House is the 'external efflorescence of the soul of the painter' is as true today as it was in 1916.

NOTES

INTRODUCTION

1. In the late 1990s, Ayako Ono was the first academic to write about how much Hornel used Japanese photographs to create his paintings. See: Ayako Ono, 'George Henry and E. A. Hornel's visit to Japan and *Yokohama Shashin*: The influence of Japanese photography', *Apollo* 150 (November 1999), pp. 11–18.
2. The terminology of Myanmar, known as Burma during British colonial rule, is complex. While both terms are still frequently used, including by those from the country, after research and consultation, we have chosen to use Myanmar. The adjective and proper noun are the same, e.g. 'Hornel's photos of Myanmar dancers, taken in Myanmar'. Where Burma is used in a quote or title, we have retained the term. Likewise, when Hornel visited Sri Lanka, it was known as Ceylon. We have made the decision to refer to it as Sri Lanka, except where quotes or painting titles specify Ceylon.
3. For ease of viewing, all the images of glass plate negatives from the Hornel collection have been presented as positives in this publication.
4. While all these photographs were in Hornel's working collection, their exact provenance is sometimes uncertain. Many of his Japanese photographs were taken by commercial photographers, only some of whom can currently be identified. Other Japanese photographs seem to have been taken more informally during what look like studio sessions or on the streets of Tokyo. Some of these were possibly taken by Hornel himself, or possibly by fellow members of the Photographic Society of Japan. It seems likely that Hornel took all the photographs in the collection from Sri Lanka and Myanmar, although it is possible some of the Sri Lankan ones came from his cousin James. Hornel worked with Robert McConchie to take his Scottish photographs and directed and posed the models himself. However, his presence in a number of the images demonstrates he did not always press the shutter.
5. Yokohama *shashin* drew heavily on earlier *ukiyo-e* woodblock prints for their subjects and composition. Judging by the pristine condition of the *ukiyo-e* books in his collection (in contrast to the heavily used photographs) Hornel does not seem to have drawn directly on *ukiyo-e*, but elements from them did make their way into his art via *shashin*.
6. We have followed the convention of not pluralising Japanese terms such as *geisha* or *kimono* with an 's'.
7. Very briefly, *geisha* were (and still are) artistic entertainers while *oiran* were high-ranking courtesans. *Geisha* were not supposed to sell sex, although there is evidence that some did. See Sheldon Garon, 'The World's Oldest Debate? Prostitution and the State in Imperial Japan, 1900–1945', *The American Historical Review* 98, no. 3 (1993), p. 713.

8. Kayo Tabei, 'E. A. Hornel's Collage Orientalism and its Influence on his Post-Victorian Works' (unpublished dissertation, University of Aberdeen, 2014), pp. 44–45.
9. Ibid., p. 46.
10. The Hornel/Hornell family seem to have taken a rather erratic approach to the spelling of their last name. Both E. A. Hornel's father, William, and his cousin James – whom he visited in Sri Lanka – spelled the name 'Hornell'. See Bill Smith, *Hornel: The Life and Work of Edward Atkinson Hornel* (Edinburgh: Atelier Books, 1997), p. 10.
11. Smith, *Hornel* (1997), pp. 17–20.
12. Just 20 years after the formal announcement of photography in 1839, photography was first officially presented at the Salon des Beaux-Arts. See Paloma Alarcó, *The Impressionists and Photography* (Madrid: Museo Nacional Thyssen-Bornemisza, 2019), p. 28.
13. Hornel's collection of Japanese volumes may have been collected in Japan, or in Scotland, or both.
14. All the photographs and paintings illustrated in this work are in the collection of the National Trust for Scotland at Broughton House & Garden, unless otherwise stated.

CHAPTER I

1. It is worth noting that the painting *Figures with Lanterns and a Bridge* (1894, Fig. 72) by Hornel appears to have used the same photograph as a model. The two may well have shared photos during their trip to Japan, or had access to the same material via the Photographic Society of Japan. See Ayako Ono's chapter.
2. Alarcó, *The Impressionists*, p. 185.
3. Ibid.
4. Malcolm Daniel, *Edgar Degas, Photographer* (New York: The Metropolitan Museum of Art, 1998), p. 41.
5. Alarcó, *The Impressionists*, p. 186.
6. Ibid.
7. Dorothy M. Kosinski, *The Artist and the Camera: Degas to Picasso* (New Haven: Yale University Press, 1999), p. 16.
8. Ibid.
9. Ibid.
10. Ayako Ono, *Japonisme in Britain: Whistler, Menpes, Henry, Hornel and Nineteenth-Century Japan* (Abingdon and New York: RoutledgeCurzon, 2003), p. 116.
11. Edward Atkinson Hornel, 'Japan' lecture delivered (by John Keppie) at the Corporation Art Galleries, Glasgow, 9 February 1895, Hornel Collection, National Trust for Scotland, Broughton House & Garden.
12. Bill Smith, *Hornel: The Life and Work of Edward Atkinson Hornel* (Edinburgh: Atelier Books, 2010), p. 142.
13. One might assume that it was his habit to get physically involved. In a letter sent during his trip to Myanmar, he briefly explains how he arranged for two dancers to pose for him: 'The photoman said he would supply two good dancing girls, if I would go & pose them … He certainly procured two very handsome & magnificently clothed females, who posed excellently & from a view of the negatives, they are a fine and useful set.' Letter from Hornel at the Miyako Hotel, Kyoto to Thomas Fraser, 25 May 1921, Hornel Collection, National Trust for Scotland, Broughton House & Garden.
14. Douglas Robert Nickel, *Dreaming in Pictures: The Photography of Lewis Carroll* (New Haven: Yale Univesity Press, 2002), p. 66.

15. John Pultz, *The Body and the Lens: Photography from 1839 to the Present* (New York: Harry N. Abrams, 1995), p. 41.
16. Anne Marsh, *The Darkroom: Photography and the Theatre of Desire* (Melbourne: Macmillan, 2003), p. 120.
17. Smith, *Hornel* (2010), p. 142.
18. Carol Jacobi, *Painting with Light: Art and Photography from the Pre-Raphaelites to the Modern Age* (London: Tate Publishing, 2016), p. 73.
19. Barbara Dayer Gallati, *Great Expectations: John Singer Sargent painting children* (New York: Bulfinch Press, 2004), p. 23.
20. Laurel Bradley, 'From Eden to Empire: John Everett Millais's *"Cherry Ripe"*', *Victorian Studies* 34, no. 2 (Winter 1991), p. 192.
21. Roger Billcliffe, *Guthrie and the Scottish Realists* (London: Fine Art Society, 1981), unpaginated.
22. Roger Billcliffe, *Pioneering Painters. The Glasgow Boys* (Glasgow: Glasgow Museums, 2010), p. 51.
23. Ayako Ono writes that Hornel 'made a good use of a European manner to recreate his original style while treating Japanese subject matter'. Or for Myanmar and Sri Lankan subject matter, one might add. Ono, *Japonisme in Britain*, p. 130.

CHAPTER 2

1. Van Gogh began life drawing classes with Verlat in January 1886. Letter from Vincent van Gogh at Antwerp to Theo van Gogh, Tuesday 19 or Wednesday 20 January 1886, Van Gogh Museum, Amsterdam, 553.
2. Letter from Vincent van Gogh at Antwerp to Theo van Gogh, Saturday 28 November 1885, Van Gogh Museum, Amsterdam, 545.
3. Ibid.
4. Frances Fowle, 'Vincent's Scottish Twin: the Glasgow Art Dealer Alexander Reid', *Van Gogh Museum Journal* (2000), p. 93.
5. 'I really don't know what you should do in the XX Brussels business' – Letter from George Henry at 4 Binnie Place to Hornel, Tuesday morning (almost certainly written in 1885, as Henry lived in Binnie Place in 1885 and by 1886 had moved to 113 West Regent Street), Hornel Collection, National Trust for Scotland, Broughton House & Garden.
6. See Bruce Laughton, 'The British and American Contributors to Les XX, 1884–1893', *Apollo* 86 (November 1967), pp. 372–79.
7. Letter from Henry at Tokyo to James Pittendrigh Macgillivray, 22 August 1893, Macgillivray Archive, National Library of Scotland, 349/31.
8. Translated literally, the Japanese word *shunga* means 'pictures of spring'; spring is a common euphemism for sex.
9. Since 1892 Henry had been suffering from a painful inflammation of the prostate which he was sure had not been caused by a sexually transmitted disease, but only because he was too poor to engage with Glasgow's prostitutes. Letter from Henry at 136 Wellington Street, Glasgow to Hornel (Hornel had lent Henry his lodgings), 30 August 1892, Hornel Collection, National Trust for Scotland, Broughton House & Garden.
10. 'Milne of Tokin who is now settled in Isle of Wight is to be in Glasgow tomorrow and perhaps Friday. I suppose he is just passing thro' – Letter from Henry to Hornel, 12 August 1896, Hornel Collection, National Trust for Scotland, Broughton House & Garden. Milne had been appointed Professor of Mining and Geology at the Imperial College of Engineering in Tokyo in March 1876. In 1881, he married Tone Horikawa, also a geologist, with whom in 1895 he settled on the Isle of Wight.

11. Letter from Henry at 136 Wellington Street, Glasgow to Hornel, undated, Hornel Collection, National Trust for Scotland, Broughton House & Garden. This letter is undated, but must be soon after their return to Scotland, as Henry mentions repaying Burton money for slides. Burton already had a two-year-old daughter, Tamako, who lived with her father and his wife. Burton's younger sister, Mary Rose Hill Burton (1857–1900), an artist who had studied in Munich and Paris, was visiting at this time and travelled through Japan with her brother.
12. In this publication, we have presented Japanese names in the body of the text in Japanese name order, with the family name first, followed by the given name.
13. Speculation that both Henry and Hornel were co-habiting with Japanese women – and that Hornel's companion had become pregnant – is founded on a highly imaginative interpretation of one letter. See Olive Checkland, *Japan and Britain After 1859: Creating Cultural Bridges* (Abingdon: Routledge, 2002), pp. 144–45.
14. Henry to Macgillivray, from Tokyo, 22 August 1893.
15. Hornel, 'Japan' lecture.
16. Ibid.
17. Henry to Macgillivray, from Tokyo, 22 August 1893.
18. Ibid.
19. Ibid.
20. It was not until 1907 that Japan established a minimum age of consent at 13 years old. See Garon, 'The World's Oldest Debate?', pp. 713 and 724.
21. Letter from Henry to Hornel, undated, Hornel Collection, National Trust for Scotland, Broughton House & Garden. Thomas Annan died in 1887 but the family business continued.

CHAPTER 3

1. On the Linked Ring, see Margaret Harker, *The Linked Ring: The Secession Movement in Photography in Britain, 1892–1910* (London: Heinemann, 1979).
2. *Japan Weekly Mail*, 27 May 1893, p. 622.
3. Ibid.
4. *Japan Weekly Mail*, 27 May 1893, p. 616.
5. 'Two Glasgow Artists in Japan: An Interview with Mr. George Henry', *Castle Douglas*, 20 July 1894, cited in Ono, *Japonisme in Britain*, p. 197.
6. Tamamura was elected a member of the Photographic Society of Japan at a meeting of 12 December 1889. See *Japan Weekly Mail*, 21 December 1889, p. 578.
7. *Japan Weekly Mail*, 17 June 1893, pp. 700–01. Tonokura Tsunetarō became the manager of the Yokohama photographic studio of A. Farsari & Co. on the departure of its eponymous founder, Adolfo Farsari (1841–1898), for Italy in 1890. The correspondent's reference to 'Tonokura of Yokohama' alludes to the exhibits submitted by A. Farsari & Co., while acknowledging the pre-eminence by this time of its Japanese manager. Tonokura remained manager of the firm until becoming its proprietor in 1901, before eventually establishing his own studio in 1904. See Sebastian Dobson, 'Yokohama shashin', in *Art & Artifice: Japanese Photographs of the Meiji Era* (Boston: MFA Publications, 2004), p. 28.
8. *Photographic Times* 23, no. 618 (21 July 1893), p. 394.
9. For more on Brinkley, see Ellen P. Conant, 'Captain Frank Brinkley Resurrected', in *Meiji no Takara / Treasures of Imperial Japan (Nasser D. Khalili Collection of Japanese Art)*, ed. Oliver Impey and Malcolm Fairley (London: The Kibo Foundation 1995), vol. 1, pp. 124–151.
10. Ono, *Japonisme in Britain*, p. 122.

11. 'Messrs. Henry and Hornel', *Japan Weekly Mail*, 5 May 1894, p. 535.
12. Ibid.

CHAPTER 4

1. Hornel, 'Japan' lecture.
2. Five letters from Henry to Hornel: at Inagi (Inage) near Chiba, 6 October 1893; at Inagi (Inage) near Chiba, dated in pencil October 1893; at Tatemachi Kanazawa, Saturday 13 January 1894; unaddressed and undated letter; a scrap of a note written on the back of half a telegram form. All Hornel Collection, National Trust for Scotland, Broughton House & Garden.
3. *Castle Douglas*, 20 July 1894, press cuttings album in the Hornel Collection, National Trust for Scotland, Broughton House & Garden.
4. Hornel, 'Japan' lecture.
5. Hornel, 'Japan' lecture. See also *The Glasgow Herald*, 11 February 1895, press cuttings album in the Hornel Collection, National Trust for Scotland, Broughton House & Garden.
6. *Glasgow Evening News*, 21 April 1893. See also Smith, *Hornel* (1997), pp. 90–91.
7. Letter from Henry at Inagi (Inage) to Hornel, October 1893.
8. Letter from Henry at Inagi (Inage) to Hornel, 6 October 1893.
9. Tatewaki Kazuo, ed., *Japan Directory* 15 (1893), p. 36 and *Japan Directory* 16 (1894), p. 34 (Tokyo: Yumani Shoboh, 1996). Also, *Shashin Shinpō* (*The Photographic News*), no. 56 (1894), p. 65. In addition, *Shashin Shinpō*, no. 53 reports that Parlett chaired the meeting of the Photographic Society of Japan held in Kyobashi on 16 March 1894.
10. Noburu Koyama, 'Arthur Morrison (1863–1945): Writer, Novelist and Connoisseur of Japanese Art', in *Britain and Japan: Biographical Portraits, Volume 7*, ed. Hugh Cortazzi (Folkestone: Global Oriental, 2010), p. 541. I am grateful to Dr Jennifer Melville for the kind information. See also Ian Ruxton, ed., *The Diaries of Sir Ernest Satow, British Minister in Tokyo (1895–1900): A Diplomat Returns to Japan* (Morrisville: Lulu Press, 2010), p. 7.
11. Letter from Captain Francis Brinkley to Hornel, 16 October 1893, Hornel Collection, National Trust for Scotland, Broughton House & Garden.
12. For further information, see Nagaoka Shozo, 'Hotel Metropole Ryakushi (A Brief History of the Hotel Metropole),' *Kindai Bunka no Genten: Tsukiji Kyoryuchi* (*The Origin of Modern Culture: Tsukiji Concession*) 1, (2000), pp. 75–83. The site is now occupied by part of St Luke's International Hospital.
13. *Castle Douglas*, 20 July 1894.
14. Hornel, 'Japan' lecture.
15. Ibid.
16. Ibid.
17. Ibid.
18. It is worth noting that all of the photos in the wood-covered album seem to be commercial photographs taken by professional photographers such as Kusakabe Kimbei (1841–1934).
19. Hornel, 'Japan' lecture.
20. Ibid.

CHAPTER 5

1. Lavery's first job was as a colourist for the photographer J. B. Macnair, who had commercial studio premises on West Nile Street in Glasgow. See John Lavery, *The Life of a Painter* (Boston: Little, Brown and Co., 1940), p. 42. James Paterson used photographs in his painting process. A collection of his photography is held in the archives at the University of Glasgow's Special Collections.

2. For more on this, see Alex D. D. Craik, 'Science and Technology in 19th Century Japan: The Scottish Connection', *Fluid Dynamics Research* 39, nos 1–3 (January–March 2007), pp. 24–48.
3. Born in Saitama, Ogawa had studied English and photography before moving to Tokyo, aged 20. Here, he was hired as an interpreter for the Yokohama Police Department. Two years later, in 1882, Ogawa took a trip to Boston where he became a professional photographer. After nearly two years in the USA, Ogawa opened the first commercial photographic studio in Tokyo. Soon after, he established a dry plate manufacturing company and Japan's first collotype business.
4. Hornel, 'Japan' lecture.
5. For more information in this area, see Nicole Coolidge Rousmaniere and Mikiko Hirayama, eds, *Reflecting Truth: Japanese Photography in the Nineteenth Century* (Amsterdam: Hotei Publishing, 2004); and Anne Tucker, *The History of Japanese Photography* (New Haven: Yale University Press, 2003).
6. Quote from *The Glasgow Herald*, 4 May 1895, no. 107. The commercial photographers extended a Japanese tradition that stems from the seventeenth century. *Bijinga* or 'pictures of beauties' became popular subject matter for artists and patrons (particularly the growing middle classes) and were produced largely as woodblock prints. These showed elegant and beautiful women, with their clothing and hair meticulously recorded, undertaking refined leisure activities. Kitagawa Utamaro (*c.*1753–1806) was one of the most highly regarded practitioners of this genre. His work was fashionable with Western collectors in the nineteenth century. His print series included: *Ten Types of Women's Physiognomies* (1792–93); *Famous Beauties of Edo* (1792–93); *Ten Learned Studies of Women* (1792–93); *Array of Supreme Beauties of the Present Day* (1794); *Flourishing Beauties of the Present Day* (1795–97); and *Ten Forms of Feminine Physiognomy* (1802).
7. For more information on this, see Eleanor M. Hight, 'The Many Lives of Beato's "Beauties"', in *Colonialist Photography: Imag(in)ing Race and Place*, eds Hight and Gary D. Sampson (Abingdon: Routledge, 2004), pp. 126–58.
8. In August 1920, Elizabeth and Hornel set off on a year-long trip, staying three months in Myanmar and then travelling on to Singapore, Hong Kong and Shanghai, before arriving in Kyoto. They spent six months in Japan then went on to Canada and America. Hornel notes in a letter that he was sent a 'fine and useful set' of photographs of the 'two very handsome and magnificently clothed females' from Japan by the 'Photoman' (who is not identified). Letter from Hornel at the Miyako Hotel, Kyoto to Fraser, 25 May 1921, Hornel Collection, National Trust for Scotland, Broughton House & Garden.
9. The exhibition ran for a month, from 24 April to 17 May. See Smith, *Hornel* (1997), pp. 96–97. *The Glasgow Herald* noted that Hornel had 40 works on show; see 'Mr Hornel's Pictures,' *The Glasgow Herald*, Saturday 4 May 1895, p. 107.
10. *Glasgow Evening News*, 25 April 1895, quoted in Smith, *Hornel* (1997), p. 96.
11. *The Studio* 9 (1896), p. 208, quoted in Smith, *Hornel* (1997), p. 97.
12. Smith, *Hornel* (1997), p. 142.

CHAPTER 6

1. Kanchanakesi Channa Warnapala, 'Dismantling the Gaze: Julia Margaret Cameron's Sri Lankan Photographs', *Postcolonial Text* 4, no. 1 (2008), p. 2.
2. Letter from Hornel at Galle to Fraser, 26 June 1907, Hornel Collection, National Trust for Scotland, Broughton House & Garden.
3. Letter from Hornel at Mandalay to Fraser, 17 December 1920, Hornel Collection, National Trust for Scotland, Broughton House & Garden.

4. The tea plantations were largely, although not exclusively, worked by immigrant Tamils from India. For a further discussion of the Sinhalese presence on the plantations see: Roland Wenzlhuemer, 'The Sinhalese Contribution to Estate Labour in Ceylon, 1881–1891', *Journal of the Economic and Social History of the Orient* 48, no. 3 (2005), pp. 442–58.
5. Wenzlhuemer, 'Indian Labour Immigration and British Labour Policy in Nineteenth-Century Ceylon', *Modern Asian Studies* 41, no. 3 (May 2007), p. 600.
6. Ibid. p. 589.
7. Ibid. p. 590.
8. Ibid. p. 592.
9. Ibid. p. 600.
10. Sahana David Menon, 'Fighting Poverty, Sri Lanka's Tea Estate Workers Demand Pay Increase', *Global Press Journal* (11 January 2017).
11. Letter from George Bernard Shaw in London to Jawaharlal Nehru, 18 September 1948, quoted in: Jawaharlal Nehru, ed., *A Bunch of Old Letters: Being Mostly Written To Jawaharlal Nehru and Some Written By Him* (London: Viking, 2005), p. 522.
12. Andrew Bank, 'Anthropology and Portrait Photography: Gustav Fritsch's "Natives of South Africa", 1863–1872', *Kronos*, no. 27 (November 2001), p. 44.
13. Allan Sekula, 'The Body and the Archive', in *The Contest of Meaning: Critical Histories of Photography*, ed. Richard Bolton (Cambridge: MIT Press, 1992), p. 345.
14. William Dalrymple, *The Age of Kali: Indian Travels and Encounters* (London: Penguin Books, 1998), p. 239.
15. Nira Wickramasinghe, *Dressing the Colonised Body: Politics, Clothing and Identity in Colonial Sri Lanka* (Hyderabad: Orient Blackswan, 2003), p. 17.
16. The full, fascinating history of the *sari* blouse, and the crucial role in its development played by Indian social reformer Jnanadanandini Devi, is unfortunately too complex to go into detail here. See for example: Mukulika Banerjee and Daniel Miller, *The Sari* (Oxford and New York: Berg, 2008), p. 254.
17. Philippa Levine, 'Naked Truths: Bodies, Knowledge, and the Erotics of Colonial Power', *Journal of British Studies* 52, no. 1 (January 2013), p. 9.

CHAPTER 7

1. Smith, *Hornel* (1997), p. 120.
2. Alice Hart, *Picturesque Burma: Past and Present* (London: J. M. Dent & Co., 1897).
3. Ibid. p. 4.
4. Ibid. pp. 3–4.
5. Ibid. p. 23.
6. Ibid. p. 154.
7. G. E. Mitton, *A Bachelor Girl in Burma* (London: Adam and Charles Black, 1907), p. 219.
8. V. C. Scott O'Connor, *The Silken East: A Record of Life & Travel in Burma* (London; Hutchinson & Co., 1904).
9. Derek Hudson, *For Love of Painting: The Life of Sir Gerald Kelly* (London: Peter Davies, 1975), p. 31.
10. Ibid. p. 32.
11. Ibid. p. 36.
12. Letters from Hornel at Mandalay to Fraser, 17 December 1920 and 5 December 1920, Hornel Collection, National Trust for Scotland, Broughton House & Garden.

13. Smith, *Hornel* (1997), pp. 120–21.
14. It is possible that Hornel would have been unable to obtain photographs of women preparing to bathe in the Irrawaddy, either for reasons of modesty on their behalf, or if it were a scene he only saw from a moving boat, making photography a challenge.

CHAPTER 8

1. Historic Environment Scotland, Charleton House, 2019, GDL00100.
2. Historic Environment Scotland, Kinloch Castle, 2019, GDL00242.
3. James Truscott, *Private Gardens of Scotland* (London: Weidenfeld and Nicolson, 1988), p.96.
4. Historic Environment Scotland, Arbigland, 2019, GDL00015.
5. Peter Clough, *Inverewe* (Edinburgh: National Trust for Scotland, 1994).
6. John Henry Dixon, *Japanese Garden, Dundarach, Pitlochry* (self-published pamphlet, Smail Archive: Dundarach Hotel, 1906).
7. Josiah Conder, *Landscape Gardening in Japan* (Tokyo: Kelly & Walsh, 1893).
8. Josiah Conder, 'The Art of Landscape Gardening in Japan', *Transactions of the Asiatic Society of Japan* 14 (1886), pp. 119–175.
9. Conder, *Landscape Gardening in Japan* p. 2.
10. Florence and Ella Du Cane, *The Flowers and Gardens of Japan* (London: Adam & Charles Black, 1908).
11. Harriet Taylour, *Japanese Gardens* (London: Methuen, 1912).
12. Herbert Ponting, 'In Lotus-Land: Picturesque Beauties of Japan Recorded by the Camera', *The Illustrated London News*, 1 June 1907, p. 825.
13. Thomas William Sanders, *The Flower Garden* (London: W. H. & L. Collingridge, 1907), p. 34.
14. Ibid, pp. 34–35.
15. P. S. Hayward, 'The Japanese Ideal,' *The Gardeners' Magazine* 52 (10 July 1909), p. 530.
16. Jiro Harada and Frank A. Lombard, *Kyoto Exhibitors' Association to the Japan–British Exhibition* (Kyoto: Kyoto Exhibitors' Association, 1910), p. 54.
17. James Shaw Simpson, 'Broughton House, Kirkcudbright, Residence of Mr Hornel', *Scottish Country Life* 3, no. 6 (June 1916), pp. 260–63.
18. Charles Godfrey Holme and Shirley B. Wainwright, *The Studio Year-book of Decorative Art* (London: The Studio, 1925), p. 181.
19. Countryside Commission for Scotland, *An Inventory of Gardens and Designed Landscapes in Scotland: Dumfries, Galloway and Strathclyde, Volume 2* (Glasgow: Land Use Consultants, 1987), p. 22.
20. Ibid.
21. Julie Rolfe, 'Scotland's Japanese Gardens', *The Pleasaunce: Scotland's Garden and Landscape Heritage*, no. 7 (February 2019), pp. 3–9.

CHAPTER 9

1. Smith, *Hornel* (1997), p. 23.
2. E. A. Taylor, 'E. A. Hornel: An Appreciation', *Kirkcudbright Academy Magazine*, Hornel Memorial Number (June 1934).
3. Letter from Hornel at 'The Studio, [Broughton House] Kirkcudbright' to Joe Hewat Esq., 3 September 1900, Hornel Collection, National Trust for Scotland, Broughton House & Garden.
4. John Keppie, 'Designs for E. A. Hornel, Esq, 8 December 1900, Broughton House, Kirkcudbright', Stewartry Museum, Kirkcudbright. In October 1901, Keppie formed the firm Honeyman, Keppie & Mackintosh with John Honeyman and Charles Rennie Mackintosh. I am grateful to Margaret Stewart of Edinburgh University for drawing attention to the potential

influence of Charles Rennie Mackintosh in the design of the parquet flooring which is the subject of ongoing research.

5. Simpson, 'Broughton House', pp. 260–61.
6. Simpson, 'E. A. Hornel, a Great Scottish Artist', *S.M.T. Magazine and Scottish Country Life* (*Leisure and Sport* segment) 8, (May 1921), p. 13.
7. John Keppie, 'Designs for E. A. Hornel, Esq, Jan 1909, Broughton House, Kirkcudbright', Hornel Collection, National Trust for Scotland, Broughton House & Garden.
8. Ian Gow, 'A Palace of Art Beside the Sea', *Apollo* 183 (April 2016), p. 60.
9. Letter from Hornel to Fraser, 1907, Hornel Collection, National Trust for Scotland, Broughton House & Garden.
10. Dorothy M. McBirnie, *Broughton House Garden*, 1926, unpublished album, Broughton House, 8/L1 SW.
11. On Hornel's works and their connection to nature, see Ysanne Holt, '"The Veriest Poem of Art in Nature": E. A. Hornel's Japanese Garden in the Scottish Borders', *Tate Papers*, no. 2 (Autumn 2004).
12. Marion Mako, *Broughton House Garden: Conception, History and Changes* (Edinburgh: National Trust for Scotland, 2006). Internal report.
13. Michael Russell, 'A Portrait of a Private Library' (unpublished dissertation, Newcastle Polytechnic School of Librarianship, 1985), p. 38.
14. Ibid. p. 7.
15. Extract of Registered Trust Disposition and Settlement by Edward Atkinson Hornel, Hewat, Dunn & Ramsay, Solicitors, Castle Douglas, dated 19 August 1920, registered 22 July 1933.
16. Letter from Hornel at Kyoto to Fraser, 7 May 1921, Hornel Collection, National Trust for Scotland, Broughton House & Garden.

SELECT BIBLIOGRAPHY

Alarcó, Paloma. *The Impressionists and Photography*. Madrid: Museo Nacional Thyssen-Bornemisza, 2019.

Bank, Andrew. 'Anthropology and Portrait Photography: Gustav Fritsch's "Natives of South Africa", 1863–1872'. *Kronos*, no. 27 (November 2001): pp. 43–76.

Billcliffe, Roger. *Guthrie and the Scottish Realists*. London: Fine Art Society, 1981.

——. *Pioneering Painters: The Glasgow Boys*. Glasgow: Glasgow Museums Publishing, 2010.

Bradley, Laurel. 'From Eden to Empire: John Everett Millais's "Cherry Ripe"'. *Victorian Studies* 34, no. 2 (Winter 1991): pp. 179–203.

Checkland, Olive. *Japan and Britain After 1859: Creating Cultural Bridges*. Abingdon: Routledge, 2002.

Clough, Peter. *Inverewe*. Edinburgh: National Trust for Scotland, 1994.

Conder, Josiah. 'The Art of Landscape Gardening in Japan'. *Transactions of the Asiatic Society of Japan* 14 (1886): pp. 119–75.

——. *Landscape Gardening in Japan*. Tokyo: Kelly & Walsh, 1893.

Countryside Commission for Scotland. *An Inventory of Gardens and Designed Landscapes in Scotland: Dumfries, Galloway and Strathclyde, Volume 2*. Glasgow: Land Use Consultants, 1987.

Craik, Alex D. D. 'Science and Technology in 19th Century Japan: The Scottish Connection'. *Fluid Dynamics Research* 39, nos 1–3 (January–March 2007): pp. 24–48.

Dalrymple, William. *The Age of Kali: Indian Travels and Encounters*. London: Penguin Books, 1998.

Daniel, Malcolm. *Edgar Degas, Photographer*. New York: The Metropolitan Museum of Art, 1998.

Dixon, John Henry. *Japanese Garden, Dundarach, Pitlochry*. Self-published pamphlet, Smail Archive: Dundarach Hotel, 1906.

Du Cane, Florence, and Du Cane, Ella. *The Flowers and Gardens of Japan*. London: Adam & Charles Black, 1908.

Fowle, Frances. 'Vincent's Scottish Twin: The Glasgow Art Dealer Alexander Reid'. *Van Gogh Museum Journal* (2000): pp. 90–99.

Gallati, Barbara Dayer. *Great Expectations: John Singer Sargent Painting Children*. New York: Bulfinch Press, 2004.

Garon, Sheldon. 'The World's Oldest Debate? Prostitution and the State in Imperial Japan, 1900–1945'. *The American Historical Review* 98, no. 3 (1993): pp. 710–32.

Gow, Ian. 'A Palace of Art Beside the Sea'. *Apollo* 183 (April 2016): pp. 56–61.

Harada, J., and Lombard, F. A. *Kyoto Exhibitors' Association to the Japan–British Exhibition, 1910*. Kyoto: Kyoto Exhibitors' Association, 1910.

Harker, Margaret. *The Linked Ring: The Secession Movement in Photography in Britain, 1892–1910*. London: Heinemann, 1979.
Hart, Alice. *Picturesque Burma: Past and Present*. London: J. M. Dent & Co., 1897.
Hayward, P. S. 'The Japanese Ideal'. *The Gardeners' Magazine* 52 (10 July 1909): p. 530.
Hight, Eleanor M. 'The Many Lives of Beato's "Beauties"'. In *Colonialist Photography: Imag(in)ing Race and Place*, edited by Hight and Gary D. Sampson, pp. 126–58. Abingdon: Routledge, 2004.
Holme, C. G., and Wainwright, S. B. *The Studio Year-book of Decorative Art*. London: The Studio, 1925.
Holt, Ysanne. '"The Veriest Poem of Art in Nature": E. A. Hornel's Japanese Garden in the Scottish Borders'. *Tate Papers*, no. 2 (Autumn 2004).
Hudson, Derek. *For Love of Painting: The Life of Sir Gerald Kelly*. London: Peter Davies, 1975.
Jacobi, Carol. *Painting with Light: Art and Photography from the Pre-Raphaelites to the Modern Age*. London: Tate Publishing, 2016.
Kazuo, Tatewaki, ed. *Japan Directory*. Tokyo: Yumani Shobo, 1996.
Kosinski, Dorothy M. *The Artist and the Camera: Degas to Picasso*. New Haven: Yale University Press, 1999.
Koyama, Noburu. 'Arthur Morrison (1863–1945): Writer, Novelist and Connoisseur of Japanese Art'. In *Britain and Japan: Biographical Portraits, Volume 7*, edited by Hugh Cortazzi, pp. 540–52. Folkestone: Global Oriental, 2010.
Laughton, Bruce. 'The British and American Contributors to Les XX, 1884–1893'. *Apollo* 86 (November 1967): pp. 372–79.
Lavery, John. *The Life of a Painter*. Boston: Little, Brown and Co., 1940.
Levine, Philippa. 'Naked Truths: Bodies, Knowledge, and the Erotics of Colonial Power'. *Journal of British Studies* 52, no. 1 (January 2013): pp. 5–25.
Marsh, Anne. *The Darkroom: Photography and the Theatre of Desire*. Melbourne: Macmillan, 2003.
Menon, Sahana David. 'Fighting Poverty, Sri Lanka's Tea Estate Workers Demand Pay Increase'. *Global Press Journal*, 11 January 2017.
Mitton, G. E. *A Bachelor Girl in Burma*. London: Adam and Charles Black, 1907.
Nagaoka Shozo, 'Hotel Metropole Ryakushi (A Brief History of the Hotel Metropole)'. *Kindai Bunka no Genten: Tsukiji Kyoryuchi (The Origin of Modern Culture: Tsukiji Concession)* 1 (2000): pp. 75–83.
Nehru, Jawaharlal, ed. *A Bunch of Old Letters: Being Mostly Written To Jawaharlal Nehru and Some Written By Him*. London: Viking, 2005.
Nickel, Douglas Robert. *Dreaming in Pictures: The Photography of Lewis Carroll*. New Haven: Yale University Press, 2002.
Ono, Ayako. *Japonisme in Britain: Whistler, Menpes, Henry, Hornel and Nineteenth-Century Japan*. Abingdon and New York: RoutledgeCurzon, 2003.
Ponting, Herbert. 'In Lotus-Land: Picturesque Beauties of Japan Recorded by the Camera'. *The Illustrated London News*, 1 June 1907.
Pultz, John. *The Body and the Lens: Photography 1839 to the Present*. New York: Harry N. Abrams, 1995.
Rolfe, Julia. 'Scotland's Japanese Gardens'. *The Pleasaunce*, no. 7 (February 2019): pp. 3–9.
Rousmaniere, Nicole Coolidge, and Hirayama, Mikiko, eds. *Reflecting Truth: Japanese Photography in the Nineteenth Century*. Amsterdam: Hotei Publishing, 2004.
Russell, Michael. 'A Portrait of a Private Library'. Unpublished dissertation, Newcastle Polytechnic School of Librarianship, 1985.
Ruxton, Ian, ed. *The Diaries of Sir Ernest Satow, British Minister in Tokyo (1895–1900): A Diplomat Returns to Japan*. Morrisville: Lulu Press, 2010.

Sanders, T. W. *The Flower Garden*. London: W. H. & L. Collingridge, 1907.
Scott O'Connor, V. C. *The Silken East: A Record of Life & Travel in Burma*. London: Hutchinson & Co., 1904.
Sekula, Allan. 'The Body and the Archive'. In *The Contest of Meaning: Critical Histories of Photography*, edited by Richard Bolton, pp. 343–89. Cambridge: MIT Press, 1992.
Simpson, James Shaw. 'Broughton House, Kirkcudbright, Residence of Mr E. A. Hornel'. *Scottish Country Life* 3, no. 6 (June 1916): pp. 260–63.
——. 'E. A. Hornel, a Great Scottish Artist'. *S.M.T. Magazine and Scottish Country Life* (*Leisure and Sport* segment) 8 (May 1921): pp. 12–13.
Smith, Bill. *Hornel: The Life and Work of Edward Atkinson Hornel*. Edinburgh: Atelier Books, 1997.
——. *Hornel: The Life and Work of Edward Atkinson Hornel*. Edinburgh: Atelier Books, 2010.
Tabei, Kayo. 'E. A. Hornel's Collage Orientalism and its Influence on his Post-Victorian Works'. Unpublished dissertation, University of Aberdeen, 2014.
Taylor, E. A. 'E. A. Hornel: An Appreciation'. *Kirkcudbright Academy Magazine*, Hornel Memorial Number (June 1934).
Taylour, Harriet. *Japanese Gardens*. London: Methuen, 1912.
Truscott, James. *Private Gardens of Scotland*. London: Weidenfeld and Nicolson, 1988.
Tucker, Anne. *The History of Japanese Photography*. New Haven: Yale University Press, 2003.
Warnapala, Kanchanakesi Channa. 'Dismantling the Gaze: Julia Margaret Cameron's Sri Lankan Photographs'. *Postcolonial Text* 4, no. 1 (2008): pp. 1–20.
Wenzlhuemer, Roland. 'Indian Labour Immigration and British Labour Policy in Nineteenth-Century Ceylon'. *Modern Asian Studies* 41, no. 3 (May 2007): pp. 575–602.
——. 'The Sinhalese Contribution to Estate Labour in Ceylon, 1881–1891'. *Journal of the Economic and Social History of the Orient* 48, no. 3 (2005): pp. 442–58.
Wickramasinghe, Nira. *Dressing the Colonised Body: Politics, Clothing and Identity in Colonial Sri Lanka*. Hyderabad: Orient Blackswan, 2003.

INDEX OF HORNEL'S PAINTINGS ILLUSTRATED IN THE TEXT

INDEX

A NOTE ON THE CONTRIBUTORS

Alix Agret is an art historian. She holds an MA in History of Art from the Courtauld Institute of Art and a PhD in Fine Arts from the Royal College of Art.

Samuel Gallacher works for the National Trust for Scotland and is responsible for Broughton House & Garden. He read history at Peterhouse, Cambridge and has a PhD in Cultural Heritage.

Luke Gartlan is Senior Lecturer in the School of Art History at the University of St Andrews. He is the author of *A Career of Japan: Baron Raimund von Stillfried and Early Yokohama Photography* (Brill, 2016).

Ayako Ono, associate professor at Shinshu University, Japan, received her MPhil and PhD from the University of Glasgow. Her interest is in the field of cross-cultural exchange between the West and Japan.

Dr Jill Raggett, Emeritus Reader in Gardens and Designed Landscapes at Writtle University College, has been studying the development and significance of the Japanese-style garden in Britain and Ireland for the last 30 years.

Heshani Sothiraj Eddleston is a Sri Lankan visual storyteller based in Edinburgh. Much of her work has focused on children's and women's rights and socio-economic and developmental issues in South Asia.